C A S E B O O K

ON
ETHICAL
PRINCIPLES
OF
PSYCHOLOGISTS

AMERICAN PSYCHOLOGICAL ASSOCIATION
WASHINGTON, DC

Library of Congress Cataloging-in-Publication Data

Casebook on ethical principles.

Rev. ed. of: Casebook on ethical standards of psychologists. c1967.
1. Psychologists—Professional ethics—Case studies.
2. Psychologists—Complaints against—Case studies.
I. American Psychological Association.   II. Casebook on ethical standards of psychologists.   [DNLM: 1. Ethics, Professional.   2. Psychology—standards.
WM 62 C337]
BF76.4.C37   1987   174'.915   87-11440
ISBN 0-912704-86-1 (pbk.)

73534

Copies may be ordered from:
Order Department
P.O. Box 2710
Hyattsville, MD 20784

Published by the American Psychological Association, Inc.
750 First Street, NE, Washington, DC 20002
Copyright 1987 by the American Psychological Association

Printed in the United States of America

CONTENTS

FOREWORD

This 1987 revision of the *Casebook on Ethical Principles of Psychologists* is the latest in a series of casebooks developed over time to illustrate the applications of the ethics code of the American Psychological Association (APA). Like its predecessors, it has been developed over time, 4 years in this instance, and represents the work of a number of persons, too many to acknowledge individually.

The work was primarily done by and under the supervision of the APA Ethics Committee. More than 12 different committee members and 3 different Chairs directly contributed to the writing and editing of this work. David H. Mills, Director of the APA Ethics Office, played a central role during this period in managing the writing, editing, and production process that led to the creation of the finished product.

Among the several APA staff members who were most involved in the research and writing necessary to this work were Carol Burroughs and Anne Rogers. Without the assistance of Donna Long of the Ethics Office the work would not have been completed. Final editorial work was done by Brenda Bryant and Heidi Kenaga of the APA Office of Publications and Communications.

Leonard D. Goodstein
October, 1987

INTRODUCTION

The ethical code of the American Psychological Association (APA) is unique among the ethical standards of professional associations in that it was developed using an empirical, critical-incident, content-analysis approach (*Ethical Standards of Psychologists*, APA, 1953). The resulting comprehensive, detailed code has been revised regularly, based on accumulated experience. Given the initial development process, no other outcome was reasonable. The latest revision of the APA code, the *Ethical Principles of Psychologists*, was adopted by the APA's Council of Representatives on January 24, 1981.

Because the original code was data based, it soon became apparent to the APA governance structure that the pool of cases that had been adjudicated over time by the APA Ethics Committee would provide a useful data base for the community of psychologists, providing data on both the serviceability and fairness of the code. This *Casebook* and its predecessors have been developed with that focus clearly in mind.

Each of the cases in this *Casebook* is drawn from the files of the APA Ethics Committee, and they are carefully disguised versions of actual decisions made by the Committee, the APA governance group charged with both overseeing the code and its enforcement. Each case describes the background of the complaint, how the complaint came to be sent to the Ethics Committee, how the case was adjudicated, and what sanctions, if any, were invoked. It is expected that this *Casebook*, like earlier ones, would furnish precedents for the Association, for future APA Ethics Committees, and for state and local ethics committees of psychologists; in addition, it would not only continue to serve an educative function for the profession as a whole but also document the efforts of the Association to police its own house.

Casual observers of the work of the APA Ethics Committee note that in most of the reported cases, the Committee adjudicates in favor of the complainant, that is, finds the psychologist "guilty." One of the reasons for this impression is that the process through which a case reaches the Committee is a rigorous one, and few frivolous or trivial cases ever reach the adjudication stage. Also, the concerns that bring a person to make a formal complaint against a professional psychologist are usually supportable, or such a complaint would not have been lodged in the first instance. Finally, the fact is that most of the cases actually adjudicated by the Committee do result in a judgment against the psychologist who was the object of the complaint. It should be noted that all adjudications are monitored for fairness and compliance with the *Ethical Principles* by the APA's General Counsel. Furthermore, all appeal proceedings involving a finding of an ethical violation involve the Counsel to assure fairness and adherence to the rules.

Most of the cases included in this edition of the *Casebook* are more recent than those included in prior editions. Virtually all of the cases were adjudicated between January 1981 and July 1986; cases adjudicated prior to January 1981 were included if it was determined that they were adjudicated according to those ethical principles not changed by the January 1981 revision of the code.

It is important to note that there are no cases illustrating Principles 9 or 10 included in the *Casebook*. This is in no way intended to diminish the importance of the research sections of the code but to reflect the fact that a separate *Casebook* on research ethics is currently being developed under the auspices of the APA Board of Scientific Affairs.

Psychology, like most professions, is ever-changing. Many of the tasks psychologists are engaged in in 1987 are rather different from those that occupied the time and energy of psychologists in 1953. Not only has psychology changed but the values and attitudes of the society have changed as well. A viable ethical code for a profession needs to reflect both the changing nature of society and of that profession. However, the code should also be cognizant of the primary purpose for its development—the protection of the consumer. The conflicts and dilemmas presented by these cases reflect the never-ending search for a balance between these two opposing forces—changing societal values and the responsibilities of the profession—a balance that can never be achieved, only worked toward.

Leonard D. Goodstein
October, 1987

PREAMBLE TO THE ETHICAL PRINCIPLES

Psychologists respect the dignity and worth of the individual and strive for the preservation and protection of fundamental human rights. They are committed to increasing knowledge of human behavior and of people's understanding of themselves and others and to the utilization of such knowledge for the promotion of human welfare. While pursuing these objectives, they make every effort to protect the welfare of those who seek their services and of the research participants that may be the object of study. They use their skills only for purposes consistent with these values and do not knowingly permit their misuse by others. While demanding for themselves freedom of inquiry and communication, psychologists accept the responsibility this freedom requires: competence, objectivity in the application of skills, and concern for the best interests of clients, colleagues, students, research participants, and society. In the pursuit of these ideals, psychologists subscribe to principles in the following areas:

1. Responsibility
2. Competence
3. Moral and Legal Standards
4. Public Statements
5. Confidentiality
6. Welfare of the Consumer
7. Professional Relationships
8. Assessment Techniques
9. Research With Human Participants
10. Care and Use of Animals.

Acceptance of membership in the American Psychological Association commits the member to adherence to these principles.

Psychologists cooperate with duly constituted committees of the American Psychological Association, in particular, the Ethics Committee, by responding to inquiries promptly and completely. Members also respond promptly and completely to inquiries from duly constituted state association ethics committees and professional standards review committees.

CASE P.1

Psychologist A widely advertised a new test to measure teenagers' academic potential and presented standardization data on 1,000 subjects, selected according to stringent sampling requirements. The publisher of her test issued press releases in which Psychologist A claimed to have revolutionized the testing of teenagers. The press releases, which aggressively challenged the usefulness and validity of several tests already in use, were picked up by major news media.

When requested to do so by the Ethics Committee, Psychologist A refused to share her raw data because of confidentiality restrictions, but she agreed to make available statistics on raw score distribution and reliability and validation studies. Two test development experts, Psychologists B and C, each tested 200 subjects using Psychologist A's new test and prescribed reliability and validation measures. Neither study replicated her results. When challenged, Psychologist A ignored their letters. Psychologists B and C then published their results in a journal and arranged for their institutions to issue joint press releases—also picked up by major news media—which reported their results and demanded that Psychologist A produce the original data. Psychologists B and C also filed individual complaints against Psychologist A, alleging violations of the Preamble and Principle 8.c. of the *Ethical Principles.*

The Ethics Committee asked Psychologist A to produce her raw data for its inspection. She refused to do so and threatened the Ethics Committee with a lawsuit.

Adjudication: *The Ethics Committee found Psychologist A in violation of the Preamble for failure to cooperate with the Committee. (It also found the psychologist in violation of Principle 8.c. for disregarding general testing principles and apparently violating standards of scientific integrity.)*

The Committee recommended to the Board of Directors that the psychologist be dropped from membership in the

2

Association for failure to cooperate with the Ethics Committee, and the Board concurred.

(Cross-reference to Principle 8.c., which instructs psychologists to indicate any reservations that exist concerning an assessment's validity.)

CASE P.2

Psychologist D, a researcher, was promoted to a position as director of a large federal installation. A graduate psychology student employed there as a technical assistant filed a complaint with the Ethics Committee, claiming that without due cause or warning Psychologist D had abruptly dismissed the student from his position. He further charged that Psychologist D had refused to meet with him to discuss the reasons for the action.

The Committee wrote to Psychologist D requesting a reply within 30 days to the allegations against him of ethical misconduct. Psychologist D ignored the first letter. His reply to the Committee's second letter was that since he no longer functioned as a psychologist but rather as an administrator, he was outside its jurisdiction. The Committee wrote to the psychologist that because he was an APA member, allegations concerning his professional conduct still fell under their jurisdiction; after he failed to respond, they moved to expel him from membership in APA for refusal to cooperate.

At this point, Psychologist D requested a hearing, which was arranged. He produced substantial evidence at the hearing that the employee in question was hired under a mutual understanding that the project—and his position— would end after 2 years. When the project ended, the installation had no new openings. He had also forwarded the employee's request for a meeting to the section head, previously the project coordinator, who could be more helpful to the employee. Psychologist D indicated that the meeting between the employee and the section head had taken place.

Adjudication: *The Committee found that Psychologist D's behavior in his role as a manager did not violate the Ethical Principles. However, his refusal to cooperate with the Com-*

mittee and his claim to be exempt from the Ethical Principles *because he was "no longer functioning as a psychologist" were serious violations of the Preamble. In lieu of expulsion, the Committee offered the psychologist a stipulated resignation for a minimum of 2 years, after which he could reapply for membership in APA. He accepted the sanction and was re-admitted at the end of 2 years.*

PRINCIPLE 1   **RESPONSIBILITY**

General Principle: In providing services, psychologists maintain the highest standards of their profession. They accept responsibility for the consequences of their acts and make every effort to ensure that their services are used appropriately.

CASE 1.GP.1

Psychologist A was a local contact for the principal investigator for the pilot study phase of a research project planned to investigate women's concepts of infidelity. Psychologist A hired an interviewer and gave her the name of the first subject, whom he had recruited. The subject agreed to an in-depth, videotaped interview with the understanding that should the project be funded, the videotape would become part of a documentary film shown on national television. The subject signed informed consent forms and was interviewed. The interviewer sent the videotape and her notes to Psychologist A, who forwarded them to the principal investigator.

Two weeks later the subject telephoned the interviewer, angrily stating that she had received a phone call from the principal investigator, a psychologist with whom she had once had a love affair. Their relationship had ended with his having accused her of infidelity. The interviewer called Psychologist A, who acknowledged that the principal investigator had suggested the subject and in doing so requested that his identity not be revealed "in order to protect the research." Psychologist A was appalled by the situation and stated that he had had no suspicion of the principal investigator's motive in suggesting this subject.

The interviewer and Psychologist A reported the incident to the Ethics Committee. In response to its inquiry, the principal investigator defended his behavior as a practical joke. He further claimed that the subject had always wanted to act in television dramas, and that this action was therefore an attempt by the principal investigator to reach a reconciliation.

Adjudication: *The Committee censured the principal investigator for irresponsible and unprofessional conduct, a violation of General Principle 1. In addition, the Committee required that he take a graduate psychology course in ethics. He accepted the censure, and after he had successfully completed the course the case was closed.*

CASE 1.GP.2

The Ethics Committee received a complaint from a former client of a psychologist alleged to have withheld a written report on the results of a battery of projective and objective personality measures, which she had administered and interpreted to the client the previous year. The complainant had instructed the psychologist by letter more than 6 weeks earlier to send the test report and raw data to a counselor with whom he was discussing career alternatives, and she had failed to do so. The complainant felt that the psychologist was behaving unethically, and that therefore the complainant was entitled to a refund of the fees he had paid to the psychologist.

In response to a letter from the Ethics Committee, the psychologist indicated that she had spoken by telephone with the counselor, who was not a psychologist and was not trained to interpret personality measures. The psychologist indicated that she had hesitated to release such sensitive information to a counselor whose training was questionable and to an office that could not assure the information's confidentiality. When she finally reached the counselor by telephone, her concerns were confirmed but she was relieved to find that the counselor wanted only a brief report on the complainant's personality style, his responses to stress, and his strengths. The psychologist had extracted this information and written a brief report, which she had sent to the counselor. The psychologist also sent to the Committee a copy of the report and her notes from the telephone conversation with the counselor.

Adjudication: *The Committee found the psychologist's behavior professionally responsible and informed both parties that there had been no violation of the* Ethical Principles. *The letter to the complainant explained further that psychologists are required to release such sensitive and confidential information only to another professional with appropriate training. In this case the ethics code may be more stringent than certain* *state laws, which do permit disclosure upon appropriate consent. In its letter to the psychologist, the Committee also suggested that the conflict might have been avoided had she clarified in advance with the client the circumstances under which the information could be released to a third party.*

Principle 1.a.

As scientists, psychologists accept responsibility for the selection of their research topics and the methods used in investigation, analysis, and reporting. They plan their research in ways to minimize the possibility that their findings will be misleading. They provide thorough discussion of the limitations of their data, especially where their work touches on social policy or might be construed to the detriment of persons in specific age, sex, ethnic, socioeconomic, or other social groups. In publishing reports of their work, they never suppress disconfirming data, and they acknowledge the existence of alternative hypotheses and explanations of their findings. Psychologists take credit only for work they have actually done.

Case 1.a.1

Several faculty members at a foreign university reviewed a colleague's publications in connection with his promotion review, and found that a number of the papers he had published in their native language appeared to be nearly verbatim plagiarisms of articles and book chapters published elsewhere in English. Because the faculty member in question was an APA member, the matter was brought to the attention of the Ethics Committee.

Adjudication: *The psychologist failed to respond to the Committee's numerous attempts to contact him. With the assistance of a translator, the Committee compared two of the psychologist's foreign language papers (submitted by the complainants) and the allegedly plagiarized English articles and became convinced that the psychologist had plagiarized both papers. Because the letters were sent by International registered mail, the Committee had reason to believe that its communications had been received and that the psychologist was willfully failing to cooperate; therefore, it voted to rec-*

ommend expulsion of the psychologist from the Association. The recommendation was approved by the Board of Directors.

(Cross-reference to the Preamble to the *Ethical Principles*, which requires psychologists to cooperate with the Ethics Committee.)

Case 1.a.2

The chair of a university-sponsored research committee became suspicious of a lengthy vita presented by a psychologist in connection with her application for a sabbatical travel grant. Upon investigation, the chair found that more than half of the nearly 80 articles listed in the vita had never been published and filed a complaint against the psychologist with the Ethics Committee.

Upon receipt of the material, the Committee charged the psychologist with a violation of Principle 1.a. for extreme exaggeration of her publication record. The psychologist responded that her vita did contain "certain inaccuracies" at the time of its submission, but that this was caused by a combination of "sloppy recordkeeping" and a disagreement with the university as to what constituted a "publication." She explained that the gross discrepancy in number partly reflected inadvertent double counting of papers submitted to more than one journal. The rest of the discrepancy was caused by listing lectures and symposia that she supposed "were not publications in the technical sense of the word." In any case, she assured the Committee that she had not intentionally exaggerated her publication record in order to receive promotions, awards, or research funds to which she was not entitled.

Adjudication: *The Committee found that the number of published articles was grossly exaggerated, that some articles evidently were never submitted to the cited journals, that some coauthors had never published with the psychologist, and that precise references to page length for nonexistent papers could not have been inadvertent errors or the result of a dispute as to what constituted a publication. The psychologist was found to be in violation of Principle 1.a., and the Board of Directors approved the Committee's recommendation that the psychologist be expelled from the Association.*

Principle 1.b.

Psychologists clarify in advance with all appropriate persons and agencies the expectations for sharing and utilizing research data. They avoid relationships that may limit their objectivity or create a conflict of interest. Interference with the milieu in which data are collected is kept to a minimum.

Case 1.b.1

Psychologist A received written permission from the school superintendent in a small city to test 9-year-old students in the school district, once she had obtained both the parents' and children's consent. The purpose of the study was to standardize a new screening measure that would identify children with learning disabilities. Halfway through the project, the superintendent of schools, caught in a political struggle between adversarial community groups, demanded data from the psychologist that would identify individual children who appeared to have learning disabilities. He wanted to use the information to justify allocations of funds to different schools. When the psychologist would not provide the data, the superintendent refused to let the psychologist continue the project. The superintendent then initiated legal action to obtain the data on the children and filed a complaint with the Ethics Committee, alleging that the psychologist had violated their agreement.

In response to the Committee's inquiry, the psychologist sent copies of the written permission from the superintendent and the methodology section of her project, which the superintendent had read and initialed as part of the written agreement. Neither the written agreement nor the methodology section dealt with how the study's results would be shared with the schools, nor was there alleged to be an oral agreement on the issue.

Adjudication: *The Ethics Committee found that the psychologist had acted in an ethical manner to safeguard the confidentiality of her data. Inasmuch as the agreement and methodology sections were silent on how the results would be shared, she had not breached the contract. However, the Committee wrote the psychologist an educative letter, advising her that she was in technical violation of Principle 1.b. for failure to clarify with the superintendent how the results were*

9

to be shared with and used by the school system. The Committee therefore urged the psychologist to state such arrangements clearly in all future agreements.

> (Cross-reference to Principle 7.e., which requires that, when conducting research in institutions or organizations, psychologists secure appropriate authorization to conduct such research. They are aware of their obligations to future research workers and ensure that host institutions receive adequate information about the research and proper acknowledgment of their contributions.)

Case 1.b.2

A physician, a Black resident in cardiology, filed a complaint with the Ethics Committee against Psychologist B, a researcher. Psychologist B was one of the principal investigators for a study of the effectiveness of certain types of stress reducers for White, Black, and Hispanic male hospital employees who suffered from essential hypertension. The employees had volunteered to be subjects.

According to the physician, Psychologist B had allowed the hospital personnel director, a close friend, to be present while nurses checked the blood pressure of Black and Hispanic subjects, but not White subjects, after stress-reducing measures. Charges of racial discrimination had recently been made against the personnel director. The physician alleged that Psychologist B had breached the confidentiality of the research subjects and added to the stress experienced by minority subjects, casting doubt on the validity of the results. She further alleged that Psychologist B's personal friendship with the personnel director constituted a conflict of interest, impairing his objectivity as a researcher.

Psychologist B replied to the Ethics Committee's inquiry that he had had a close working relationship with the personnel director for more than 10 years, but he did not feel that this created a conflict of interest or limited his objectivity as a researcher. He stated that specially trained nurses whom he supervised actually gathered the data, which were kept confidential. He admitted that on two occasions he had permitted the personnel director, who had expressed interest in the stress-reducing techniques, to be present during the data collection, but he claimed that these were brief visits. He denied that because the research subjects were hospital employees it was necessary to keep their identity confidential. Nor did he consider the racism charges against the personnel director to be consequential to the validity of the research or his objectivity as a researcher. He admitted that, in retrospect, allowing anyone to observe data gathering during this type of study was perhaps poor judgment.

Adjudication: *The Ethics Committee found Psychologist B in violation of Principle 1.b. in that he had failed to keep the experimental milieu free of interference, to the extent possible. He accepted censure by the Ethics Committee without further contest.*

Principle 1.c.

Psychologists have the responsibility to attempt to prevent distortion, misuse, or suppression of psychological findings by the institution or agency of which they are employees.

Case 1.c.1

An attorney, representing a man who had been convicted of murder and sentenced to life imprisonment, filed a complaint on behalf of his client against Psychologist C, an employee of the criminal justice system, who had appeared as an expert witness for the prosecution and whose testimony was an important factor in conviction. Psychologist C was specifically alleged to have suppressed test results adverse to her position.

At issue was the defendant's mental and physical condition, specifically, whether he had the ability to plan and execute the acts of which he was accused. The results of an extensive battery of tests performed by another psychologist employed within the criminal justice system had raised reasonable doubts that the accused could have committed the crime. Psychologist C had mentioned neither these tests nor their results in her testimony, although they had been made known to her before the trial. The accused could not afford to retain his own expert witness, and his legal counsel was unaware of the tests prior to the trial and was therefore unable to rebut Psychologist C's testimony.

Learning subsequent to the trial that the tests existed, the defense attorney prevailed upon two leading forensic psychologists to evaluate the test findings and the testimony of Psychologist C independently. Both psychologists concurred that the tests and their interpretation were germane to the essential elements of the crime and that Psychologist C had suppressed relevant test findings adverse to her position.

The Ethics Committee charged Psychologist C with a violation of Principle 1.c. In response to the Committee, Psychologist C claimed that she had no confidence in the tests and therefore did not mention the results. The Committee questioned her further about the theoretical or technical bases for her judgment and about her justification for ignoring disconfirming information instead of raising these issues at trial. Psychologist C did not respond directly to these questions but claimed that the two forensic psychologists were known to be partial to criminal defendants as a class and that their testimony represented a particular political group's effort to reopen the case.

Adjudication: *The Ethics Committee found that the psychologist had failed to respond adequately to the charge and was in violation of Principle 1.c. for suppressing data that were important and germane to the trial. The Committee recommended to the Board of Directors that the psychologist be dropped from membership in the Association, and the Board concurred.*

(Cross-reference to Principle 1.a., which requires psychologists to provide a thorough discussion of the limits of their findings and to acknowledge disconfirming data.)

Case 1.c.2

A psychologist was hired by a textile mill to perform a survey on the morale of company employees and report the results to management. He completed the study and conveyed the findings to management, which decided not to release them publicly. The union local, however, heard rumors about the study and discovered that it had been performed and that the mill management had suppressed the results. The president of the local tried to obtain the results from the management and when that failed contacted the psychologist. He would not comply with her request, explaining that his contract with management would not permit his release of the data. The union president then submitted a complaint against the psychologist with the APA Ethics Committee.

In response to the inquiry from the Committee, the psychologist explained that he had a contractual obligation to deliver the data only to the mill's management. He added, however, that he felt strongly that his study's findings should also have been released to employees and to their union. The psychologist supplied the Committee with copies of the correspondence he had written to management and documentation of his telephone calls, which indicated his efforts to persuade management both to release the data and to correct the serious morale problem his survey had uncovered.

Adjudication: *The Ethics Committee found no violation of the* Ethical Principles *in the psychologist's conduct but cautioned him to be more careful in the future in initially contracting with clients to prevent, if possible, his losing control so completely of the disposition of his findings. The Committee noted that it understood that psychologists in proprietary positions with industrial clients are not always in a position to dictate the use of data; however, the Committee felt that the psychologist could have been more sensitive to potential problems before initiating the survey.*

Principle 1.d.

As members of governmental or other organizational bodies, psychologists remain accountable as individuals to the highest standards of their profession.

Case 1.d.1

A case against Psychologist G was opened by the Ethics Committee *sua sponte* (on its own motion) when it came to the Committee's attention that the psychologist had been delicensed in his state of residence. In response to the Committee's letter "to show cause why he should not be expelled from the Association," Psychologist G informed the Committee that he had pleaded *nolo contendere* (no contest) to charges that he had misused research funds while employed by a federally funded program. He presented himself as an unwitting dupe in a series of kickbacks made to his employees by other persons. He denied either knowing about these kickbacks or profiting from them. Psychologist G had been indicted by a grand jury and found guilty of violating federal law. The original felony indictment had been reduced to a misdemeanor to which he had entered the *nolo contendere* plea. At this point, the state licensing body had initiated delicensing proceedings, against which Psychologist G claimed to have been "too emotionally drained" to defend himself. When the matter reached the Committee, the evidence that supported his statements was in the public domain and was reviewed by the committee members.

Adjudication: *Although empowered to recommend expulsion in cases of delicensure, the Committee recommended a stipulated resignation. It based its opinion on the fact that although Psychologist G may have been the "fall guy" for a number of corrupt suppliers, the investigator remains responsible for overseeing the conduct of his research assistants. The resignation carried the stipulation that he not reapply for membership for 5 years.*

(Cross-reference to Principle 9.c., which maintains that the investigator is responsible for ensuring ethical practice in research.)

Case 1.d.2

A psychologist employed by a state hospital charged her supervisor, Psychologist H, with unethical conduct in arbitrarily reducing the individual therapy treatment available to patients in order to increase the number of group and workshop sessions. She stated that, as a consequence, several clients had deteriorated substantially.

Psychologist H replied to the Ethics Committee's inquiry that she had reduced individual therapy in response to "administrative issues." Upon investigation, these administrative issues were revealed to be the hospital administrator's preference for group rather than individual therapy services. Psychologist H justified her actions as pursuant to orders from the hospital administrator, who was not a psychologist, and abdicated any professional responsibility to consider or recommend to the administrator other courses of action.

Adjudication: *The Ethics Committee found Psychologist H in violation of Principle 1.d. for failure to accept her accountability to the highest standards of the profession; in violation of General Principle 6 for failing to take responsibility for the client's welfare; and in violation of Principle 6.c. for failing to recognize, clarify, and take appropriate action concerning an actual or potential conflict between the demands of her employer and her professional responsibility as a psychologist. The psychologist was censured.*

(Cross-reference to Principle 3.d., which requires that psychologists attempt to resolve conflicts between Association standards and organizational practices; to General Principle 6, which mandates that psychologists protect the welfare of clients; and to Principle 6.c., which requires psychologists to clarify and make known any conflict between an organization's demand and the *Ethical Principles.*)

Principle 1.e.

As teachers, psychologists recognize their primary obligation to help others acquire knowledge and skill. They maintain high standards of scholarship by presenting psychological information objectively, fully, and accurately.

Case 1.e.1

A 4th-year graduate student charged her advisor, Psychologist E, with violation of Principle 1.e. for allegedly having impeded her progress through a doctoral program in counseling psychology. She charged specifically that he had actively discouraged practicum sites from accepting her application for openings, although such practicum experience is a prerequisite for placement in internships. The complainant further charged that, on several occasions, Psychologist E had made derogatory statements about her in public.

Psychologist E replied candidly to the Ethics Committee's inquiry that he found this student difficult to work with because of her abrasive and adversarial style. He had requested that she be assigned to another advisor, but because no faculty member

15

would accept her, the program director had asked him to continue as her advisor. He could not support her application for practicum placements because he felt she was not suited to work with clients and would reflect poorly on the program. He also admitted that several times he had become so exasperated by her comments that he had been unduly sharp.

The Ethics Committee inquired further of Psychologist E whether the counseling program or psychology department had formal procedures for dealing with students who presented such difficulties and, if so, whether Psychologist E had invoked them. Psychologist E replied that procedures did exist but were so involved and arduous that he and the program director had decided to let matters ride, in the hope that the student would reach the point where she would withdraw from the program.

Adjudication: *The Committee concluded that Psychologist E and the program director, specifically, and the departmental faculty, generally, were guilty of markedly irresponsible behavior toward the student, neglecting to help her either acquire professional skills and training or move elsewhere. The Committee found Psychologist E in violation of Principle 1.e., censured him, and required that he rectify the situation with the student and inform the Committee of the steps he was taking and their outcome. Several committee members felt that the program director should also be censured, but he had not been charged.*

Psychologist E accepted the censure and informed the Committee that the program director, at the direction of the department chair, had called a faculty meeting and planned how to approach the student. Psychologist E then had a long conference with the student and he offered her the opportunity to choose as her advisor the most senior woman faculty member. He also urged her to enter individual psychotherapy. In addition, he established a formal reevaluation date, at which time if the student were making satisfactory progress, her advisor would refer her for a pre-internship clerkship. The student accepted the terms of the agreement, and the case was closed.

(Cross-reference to Principle 7.c., which requires that psychologists who employ or supervise other professionals or professionals in training accept the obligation to facilitate the further professional development of these individuals. They provide appropriate working conditions, timely evaluations, constructive consultation, and experience opportunities.)

Case 1.e.2

Several psychology graduate students jointly charged a graduate department colloquium speaker, Psychologist X, a well-known senior psychologist in brain sciences, with violation of Principle 1.e. for presenting a controversial topic in a prejudiced, inaccurate, and subjective manner. Submitting a copy of the paper to the Ethics Committee, they claimed that the speaker had lectured on the cognitive implications of sexual differences between male and female graduate students. He had observed that in his experience, male graduate psychology students tended to prepare more rigorous experimental theses, and female graduate psychology students were more likely to produce less scientifically rigorous or significant theses.

Psychologist X ascribed this phenomenon to brain and biological differences, brushing aside the hypothesis that these tendencies might result from cultural differences in the expectations and training to which male and female children are subjected. The students further complained that the speaker, during the lecture and in subsequent informal discussion, dismissed questions that raised issues concerning Psychologist X's basic premise as well as contrary evidence published in women's studies publications.

Psychologist X replied angrily to the Ethics Committee's inquiry, claiming that the charge constituted censorship and infringement of academic freedom. He complained to the APA Board of Scientific Affairs, which advised him to try to resolve the matter with the Ethics Committee; if he could not, the Board said it would consider the matter.

Psychologist X then responded to the Committee that, in his presentation, he had espoused a developing idea that he hoped to research. Furthermore, he stated that he had read the work of the "cultural apologists," among whom he included women's studies groups, and found their presentations so biased and unscientific that to cite these arguments would grant an unmerited standing to their work.

Adjudication: *The Ethics Committee found Psychologist X in violation of Principle 1.e. for failing to present the current* *status of a controversial issue fully and objectively and issued a reprimand. A member of the Committee, a well-known research psychologist, with the Committee's approval wrote a "Dear Colleague" letter to Psychologist X dealing in some detail with the state of scientific knowledge concerning male/female traits and abilities. Psychologist X did not challenge the reprimand.*

Principle 1.f.

As practitioners, psychologists know that they bear a heavy social responsibility because their recommendations and professional actions may alter the lives of others. They are alert to personal, social, organizational, financial, or political situations and pressures that might lead to misuse of their influence.

Case 1.f.1

A former client of Psychologist F filed a complaint with the Ethics Committee, alleging that Psychologist F, a career placement counselor in private practice, had insistently advised him to apply for middle management corporate positions, despite indications to the contrary from the client's employment history—including a forced resignation—and the results of standardized tests administered by the psychologist. The client told the Committee that, because of the pressure from Psychologist F and his own lack of self-confidence, he had followed Psychologist F's advice for approximately 9 months. During that time he encountered a continuous stream of painful rejections in his job search, which prolonged the period of unemployment, depleted his financial resources, and placed considerable strain on him and his marriage. Only after discontinuing sessions with Psychologist F and initiating consultation with another counselor was the complainant able to find an appropriate position. The new psychologist validated the client's perception that the direction of Psychologist F's advice was inappropriate and encouraged him to file a complaint with the Ethics Committee.

The Committee charged Psychologist F with possible violations of Principles 1.f. and 2.e. Psychologist F replied that she was aware of the difficulties the client had encountered in his job search; however, she felt that the client had been the victim of poor management policies and was competent to handle the type of position from which he had just been forced to resign. The psychologist also attributed less dramatic difficulties in prior positions to the client's lack of self-confidence. She therefore advised the client to seek a similar position in which he could regain his confidence and eventually perform successfully. When the Committee inquired about the allegedly extreme pressure placed on the client, Psychologist F said that she felt that the client's distress about the forced resignation and anxiety concerning his judgment required the psychologist to assume a more directive role with this client than was her usual practice. She also felt that the client's idea of seeking another type of employment situation was counterproductive and admitted that she "probably discouraged him from doing so."

The Ethics Committee also asked Psychologist F to explain the apparent contradiction between her placement advice and the complainant's test results. The psychologist admitted ignoring some test results, stating that she was under financial pressure to place the complainant in a position more remunerative than those for which the complainant might have been better suited.

Adjudication: *The Committee found Psychologist F in violation of Principle 1.f., censured her, and placed her practice under the supervision of a psychologist chosen by the Committee.*

> (Cross-reference to Principle 2.e., which requires that decisions by psychologists based on test results reflect an understanding of psychological measurement.)

Case 1.f.2

Mr. and Mrs. Q were in the midst of rancorous divorce proceedings. They were unable to reach any agreement as to the custody arrangements for their one child, a 3-year-old boy. The attorney for Mr. Q hired Psychologist C to evaluate Mr. Q's fitness for custody of the boy.

Psychologist C interviewed Mr. Q on more than one occasion and performed evaluative tests during those sessions. She also tested and evaluated the boy. Mrs. Q learned of the psychologist's involvement only after her son asked her why Psychologist C was asking so many questions. She then telephoned the psychologist and asked for an appointment, but Psychologist C refused to talk with her. Mrs. Q's attorney then attempted to talk with Psychologist C but was also refused; Psychologist C insisted that to meet with either Mrs. Q or her attorney would be a breach of confidentiality with her client, Mr. Q.

At the custody hearing Psychologist C was called to testify by Mr. Q's attorney. The psychologist reported her interpretation of the results of her evaluations of Mr. Q and his son. In her testimony, she stated that her assessment indicated Mr. Q to be the relatively superior parent and recommended that primary custody be granted to Mr. Q.

At her attorney's urging, Mrs. Q filed a complaint with the Ethics Committee against Psychologist C. In response to the Committee's inquiry, Psychologist C offered a detailed and thorough explanation of the tests and interview procedures she had conducted with Mr. Q and the boy. She explained her refusal to meet Mrs. Q or her attorney as being motivated by her concern that to do otherwise would breach the ethics code by failing to respect the confidentiality due her client, Mr. Q.

Adjudication: *The Ethics Committee found Psychologist C in violation of Principle 1.f. of the* Ethical Principles *and censured her. Her procedures in interviewing Mr. Q and his son were adequate for an evaluation of the father and son; these procedures did not provide any basis, however, for the psychologist's pronouncements concerning the relative merits of Mr. and Mrs. Q as parents. She could not possibly judge Mrs. Q's fitness as a parent when she had never even spoken with her. Moreover, her refusal to see Mrs. Q could easily be construed to mean that she was improperly influenced by the source of payment for her services, that is, her assessment was clearly and unfairly prejudiced toward Mr. Q.*

PRINCIPLE 2   **COMPETENCE**

General Principle: The maintenance of high standards of competence is a responsibility shared by all psychologists in the interest of the public and the profession as a whole. Psychologists recognize the boundaries of their competence and the limitations of their techniques. They only provide services and only use techniques for which they are qualified by training and experience. In those areas in which recognized standards do not yet exist, psychologists take whatever precautions are necessary to protect the welfare of their clients. They maintain knowledge of current scientific and professional information related to the services they render.

CASE 2.GP.1

A 35-year-old woman with a diagnosis of psychomotor epilepsy and multiple personality disorder complained that she had recently discovered that Psychologist Y, who had treated her for the past 4 years, had had no prior training or supervised experience working with individuals with a multiplicity of disorders such as hers. During treatment the client's condition had become worse, and eventually she had to be hospitalized. The client charged the psychologist with practicing outside her areas of competence in violation of General Principle 2.

Psychologist Y responded to the Ethics Committee that she had begun seeing the client during the first year of her licensure as an employee of a community mental health center. There, two clinic consultants performed extensive supervision of her work: a neurologist from the public hospital seizure clinic, who controlled the client's medication, and a psychiatrist supervisor at the clinic, who was considered experienced in treating multiple personality disorders. The client made very slow progress from the outset. During the third year of their work, Psychologist Y decided to start a private practice in her home and took a part-time position at the clinic. Her supervising psychiatrist recommended that the client stay with the clinic. The clinic administrator, however, who was not a psychologist, recommended that Psychologist Y continue to work with the client in her private practice so as not to disrupt treatment. Therapy fees would be covered by Medicaid. The client agreed to this arrangement.

Psychologist Y set up weekly appointments, following their established clinic routine, and arranged with the same psychiatrist for private consultation as needed. Therapy went well for about 6 months, but then the client began to become increasingly angry during sessions, missed sessions and blamed her other personalities, and "disappeared" for several weeks at a time. Psychologist Y sought consultation from the neurologist and psychiatrist, both of whom thought that the client was decompensating and would need hospitalization. A week later, the client telephoned Psychologist Y late at night and told her that she planned to kill herself because she felt so hopeless, and she blamed her therapist for not helping her. Psychologist Y called the police, who brought the client to the county psychiatric hospital emergency room, where Psychologist Y met and stayed with her until she was admitted. Psychologist Y visited the client weekly in the hospital for therapy sessions until the client refused to see her. Upon release, the client requested a referral back to the community mental health clinic, where she was again in treatment at the time of the complaint.

In response to the complaint, Psychologist Y stated that she believed that she had acted responsibly and professionally in working with the client. She emphasized her continuous consultative arrangements with the psychiatrist. In addition, she pointed to the fact that the clinic administrator had suggested that she take the client into her private practice for the well-being of the client. She did admit, however, that she had been unable to maintain consistent contact with the neurologist since the neurologist was busy and only on contract with the mental health center.

Adjudication: *The Ethics Committee found Psychologist Y in violation of General Principles 1 and 2. Despite good intentions, she had attempted to function well beyond the limits of her experience and competence and had made a mistaken judgment in assuming that, with so little clinical experience, she could treat so disturbed a patient in private practice without the ready consultation and safeguards available in a more structured setting. As the supervising psychiatrist had advised, the client's interests would have been better served by her* *remaining at the clinic where there were staff trained to deal with her kind of problem. Moreover, by shifting responsibility for the decision to other parties, none of whom were psychologists, she had attempted to avoid accepting full responsibility for the consequences of her actions.*

Psychologist Y was censured with the stipulation that she take two advanced courses, one in organic disturbances and the second in the diagnosis and treatment of borderline personality and multiple personality disorders. She accepted the censure and stipulations.

(Cross-reference to General Principle 1, which requires psychologists to take responsibility for the consequences of their acts.)

CASE 2.GP.2

Psychologist N charged Psychologist P, a new Ph.D. in social psychology, with practicing beyond his area of competence. Psychologist P had applied for and received a license, on the basis of 2 years' experience doing research in a private mental hospital, and then opened an office to practice psychotherapy. Further, the private mental hospital's administrator, a businesswoman, had appointed Psychologist P chief psychologist, a title that Psychologist P was using as a credential.

Psychologist P replied to the Ethics Committee's charges that the state license in psychology was generic; therefore, there were no limits on how he could practice. He also claimed that his work at the mental hospital had amply prepared him to practice psychotherapy and act as chief psychologist. He attributed the complaint by Psychologist N to professional jealousy.

Adjudication: *The Ethics Committee found Psychologist P in violation of General Principle 2 and Principle 2.a. for practicing or attempting to practice outside his area of competence. The members voted to censure him with the stipulation that he withdraw from the practice of psychotherapy and cease and desist using the title of chief psychologist. He did not reply to the censure and stipulation. The Committee therefore recommended to the Board of Directors that he be dropped from membership in the Association for violation of* *the above principles as well as a violation of the Preamble for failure to cooperate.*

(Cross-reference to Principle 2.a., which mandates that psychologists accurately represent their competence, education, training, and experience, and to the Preamble to the *Ethical Principles*, which requires psychologists to cooperate with the Ethics Committee.)

Principle 2.a.

Psychologists accurately represent their competence, education, training, and experience. They claim as evidence of educational qualifications only those degrees obtained from institutions acceptable under the Bylaws and Rules of Council of the American Psychological Association.

Case 2.a.1

An attorney, representing an insurance company that was contesting the payment of claims for an extensive psychological examination and therapy, charged that Psychologist A had falsely represented herself as a clinical psychologist trained in personality assessment. The attorney alleged that the psychologist, although licensed to practice in the state on the basis of having a master's degree in experimental psychology, had obtained clinical training and her Ph.D. from a nonaccredited university. Furthermore, her academic records indicated no evidence of coursework, training, or supervised experience in personality assessment. In addition, the attorney reported that their claims reviewer had observed that the mental health treatment reports the company received from Psychologist A were virtually identical to each other.

Ms. A responded to the Ethics Committee that she was an Associate of APA and that her application for that status clearly stated that her degree was a master's in psychology from a terminal program in a regionally accredited university. She had obtained further training through a nonaccredited Ph.D. clinical psychology program, which she realized APA did not recognize. (The program consisted primarily of reading projects with 6 weeks a year in residence.) She had, however, subse-

CASEBOOK ON ETHICAL PRINCIPLES OF PSYCHOLOGISTS

quently performed "postdoctoral" work through an internship at a local psychiatric hospital. She thought that so long as "Ph.D." did not appear on her stationery, she had not violated APA policy; however, Ms. A. acknowledged that she did use the title "clinical psychologist" on her stationery to denote the area of her practice.

Adjudication: *The Ethics Committee considered two issues. First, Ms. A was licensed and therefore legally able to practice in her state. Secondly, although she did not claim to have a Ph.D. degree in either the* APA Membership Directory *or on her stationery, she nonetheless presented herself to the public as a clinical psychologist. The Ethics Committee found Ms. A in violation of General Principle 2 and Principle 2.a. because her degree was from a nonaccredited university and from a psychology program that did not meet minimal requirements for clinical training, a situation clearly at variance with the APA* Specialty Guidelines *criteria for the use of the title "clinical psychologist."*

Although Ms. A's behavior was in serious violation of professional standards, the Committee voted, in lieu of dropping her from membership, to offer Ms. A a stipulated resignation with the requirement that she not be permitted to reapply for associate status, unless she either cease presenting herself to the public as a clinical psychologist or obtain the required training at a regionally accredited university with an APA-accredited program in clinical psychology. Ms. A did not respond to the Committee's letter indicating her willingness to accept the stipulations. After she failed to respond despite adequate opportunity to do so, she was also charged with a violation of the Preamble to the Ethical Principles *for noncooperation, and the Committee then recommended to the Board of Directors that she be dropped from membership in the Association. The Board approved this recommendation.*

(Cross-reference to General Principle 2, which demands that psychologists recognize the boundaries of their competence, and to the Preamble to the *Ethical Principles*, which requires psychologists to cooperate with the Ethics Committee.)

Case 2.a.2

A state licensing board for psychology found Psychologist B guilty of representing himself to the public as a physician. He had circulated cards with an "M.D." after his name and had prescribed medication for his patients on several occasions. On the basis of a violation of Principle 2.a., the state board suspended his license for 3 years and ordered him to take corrective measures.

Upon notification of the board's actions, the Ethics Committee wrote to Psychologist B, giving him 60 days to show cause why he should not be expelled from the Association.

Psychologist B responded and offered the following arguments against expulsion. First, he had complied with all the corrective actions required by the state board. Second, at the time of the offense he was newly associated with a multidisciplinary practice; a clinic employee had printed the cards and prescription pads in error. Third, waiting for the new cards, he allowed the inaccurate ones to be distributed so that he could contribute to the practice as required by his contract; he intended to explain the error to any clients who came to him for services. Fourth, he prescribed the medication out of concern for his patients while all the psychiatrist associates were out of town for a professional meeting. Accompanying his response were letters from several psychiatrist associates corroborating his story and indicating that he had prescribed medication without malice, out of concern for his patients.

Adjudication: *After lengthy deliberations on the case, the Ethics Committee decided that the violations were very serious and Psychologist B had demonstrated extremely poor judgment, although the committee was convinced that he had not acted to harm his patients. However, despite his good intentions he had clearly operated outside of his area of competence when he had prescribed medication for patients. The Committee voted to expel him from membership in the American Psychological Association, and the Board of Directors concurred.*

(Cross-reference to Principle 4.j., under which psychologists accept the obligation to correct others who misrepresent their professional qualifications.)

Principle 2.b.

As teachers, psychologists perform their duties on the basis of careful preparation so that their instruction is accurate, current, and scholarly.

Case 2.b.1

The Ethics Committee opened a complaint *sua sponte* (on its own motion) against a university professor on the basis of a series of newspaper articles concerning a "psychology of sex" course that the psychologist had taught for the previous 10 years. The articles alleged that she gave extra credits to students who engaged in sexual experiences, analyzed these experiences, and reported on them to the class. It was not alleged that the professor had herself engaged in sexual relationships with students.

The university placed the psychologist, a tenured professor, on administrative leave while the alleged conduct was under investigation. The Ethics Committee wrote to the psychologist, asking her about the course.

The psychologist submitted considerable documentation in response, indicating that the content and procedures of the course had been approved by the psychology department, cleared through the university human subjects/ethics committee, and reviewed by the dean's office. She claimed to be the target of an extreme fundamentalist group, which had already destroyed the women's studies program. Viewing this group's activities as a serious attack on academic freedom, the psychologist offered confirming letters from the chair of the university ethics committee and the former director of the defunct women's studies program.

Moreover, she alleged that the newspaper articles misrepresented the course requirements. Rather than require students to engage in "new" or "experimental" sexual experiences, she gave extra credit for various activities, including research papers, critiques of research, and personal accounts of past sexual experiences. Neither engaging in sexual experiences nor reporting on these in class was a requirement. Although some academic majors required the course, the psychologist did not feel that subjecting students to personal discussions involving sexuality was inappropriate or unethical, in that a course goal was to teach students to have a healthy attitude toward sex and to discuss it openly and honestly.

Adjudication: *The Ethics Committee reviewed the course syllabus and course catalogue description, finding that the psychologist's instruction in sexuality appeared to be accurate, current, and, for the most part, scholarly. The documentation appeared to corroborate her statements that relevant university channels had cleared the course. Some committee members felt that verbal reports in an undergraduate class of sexual experiences served questionable educational purposes and could be construed instead to satisfy prurient interests. The final disposition was that the evidence did not indicate an ethical violation.*

Case 2.b.2

The mother of a 17-year-old college freshman wrote a letter of complaint to the Ethics Committee concerning her daughter's psychology teacher, Psychologist T. The mother, a physician, was alarmed that Psychologist T was teaching a section on hypnosis in the introductory psychology course and urging his students to volunteer to be subjects for hypnotic induction for extra credit. The student's mother had inquired into Psychologist T's credentials and could not determine that he had any professional training in hypnosis. The complainant also thought—on the basis of the assigned readings—that Psychologist T had not presented the limitations and dangers of hypnosis and judged his handling of the topic to be adventuristic and unscholarly. The complainant had first written to the psychology department chair, who replied that faculty members enjoyed academic freedom and wide latitude in determining the content of their courses.

Psychologist T replied to the Ethics Committee that he did indeed devote a section of his introductory psychology course to hypnosis and hypnotic regression, as a way to stimulate student interest in altered states of consciousness and unconsciousness, and that he did offer extra credit to students willing to be subjects in his experiments on hypnosis. Each experiment was carefully reviewed and accepted by the university's human subjects committee. In addition, he submitted a copy of his syllabus, in which the history of hypnosis, its limitations and dangers, and the results of experiments using hypnosis, were clearly presented. He claimed that several years of postdoctoral training in experimental hypnosis sufficiently qualified him to perform these experiments.

Adjudication: *On the basis of the information submitted, the Ethics Committee found insufficient evidence to sustain a violation of Principle 2.b.; however, they did express concern about the possible effects of hypnotic experiences on students and urged that Psychologist T use considerable caution in selecting subjects. Several Committee members were also concerned about the self-serving and potentially coercive nature of offering extra credit for participating in experiments run by Psychologist T. They suggested that it would be more appropriate to give extra credit for participating in any psychology department experiment for which human subjects were sought.*

(Cross-reference to Principle 1.f., which requires psychologists to be alert to pressures that might induce them to misuse their influence.)

Principle 2.c.

Psychologists recognize the need for continuing education and are open to new procedures and changes in expectations and values over time.

Case 2.c.1

Mrs. A filed a complaint against her husband's psychotherapist, Psychologist Z, charging him with holding and conveying to her husband extremely outdated ideas and values concerning women and the marital relationship. Her husband had entered treatment with Psychologist Z because of a depressive reaction following the death of his father. Six months into therapy, her husband had requested that she attend a series of sessions with him because of difficulties they were beginning to have in their relationship. She was eager to participate but was chagrined to discover that a probable source of the friction was Psychologist Z himself. She told the Committee that Psychologist Z had an "old-fashioned" view that a man's position was to be the unquestioned patriarchal head of the family, and a woman was required to be subservient and obedient. She had asked Psychologist Z whether he had read about the women's movement and the need to equalize relationships between men and women, and he had then expressed concern lest she be a "radical feminist," because he felt that this would be detrimental to any male/female relationship. She also offered quotes to indicate that Psychologist Z's attitude about sexual relationships indicated inadequate knowledge of female sexuality. She further stated that Psychologist Z disapproved of any woman having a career and, therefore, viewed her career as a handicap to the marriage.

The complainant had refused to continue the joint sessions, and several months later, her husband terminated therapy with Psychologist Z. She summarized her position by indicating that she felt that Psychologist Z had helped her husband through the loss of his father but had adversely affected their marital relationship. Had she not held clearly to her own convictions and persuaded her husband of the error in Psychologist Z's position, their marriage might have been destroyed. The complainant indicated that she filed the complaint out of concern that someone as influential as a psychologist and therapist could be unaware that his attitudes were so out of keeping with the times and consequently cause much harm to other clients.

The Ethics Committee requested information from Psychologist Z about his initial training and continuing education as well as a response to the complainant's allegations. He indicated that he had attended numerous continuing education workshops over the years on various therapeutic techniques but had not thought extensively about the issues the complainant raised until his work with her. He had since realized the merit of her criticisms and begun studying recent books on the psychology of women. He also planned to attend any workshops offered on related topics at the next APA convention.

Adjudication: *The Committee found Psychologist Z in technical violation of Principle 2.c. However, on the basis of his reply that he had not been aware of the need to update his knowledge about the psychology of women but was now taking steps to do so, a majority voted to close the case with an educative letter but without further action.*

Case 2.c.2

An acrimonious exchange of letters to the editor was published in a professional journal having to do with the diagnosis and treatment of children's difficulties. Psychologist A, in response to an article concerning the extent to which hyperactivity in children has a psychodynamic rather than neurophysiological basis, stated that in the past she had tended to view hyperactivity as a reactive behavior disorder that reflected family pathology. In light of this article and other recent publications, she had fundamentally realigned her thinking to view hyperactivity in children as primarily neurophysiological in origin, unless sufficient psychodynamic evidence is gathered to indicate otherwise.

Psychologist B wrote a caustic letter that attacked Psychologist A for abandoning psychodynamic interpretation, in which he stated that hyperactivity and most learning difficulties in children were psychodynamic in origin. Psychologist B claimed further that to view these problems otherwise constituted an attack by forces hostile to psychodynamic interpretations.

Psychologist A filed a complaint with the Ethics Committee charging Psychologist B with unprofessional conduct in his public statements and with failing to consider new ideas in child diagnosis and treatment. She submitted to the Ethics Committee copies of the original article and the published letters to the editor. Prior to filing the complaint, Psychologist A had written privately to Psychologist B and expressed the same concern about his behavior. Her letters had apparently been ignored.

Adjudication: *The Ethics Committee deliberated as to whether the statements made by Psychologist B in this heated exchange constituted a violation of Principle 2.c. It decided not to open a case and instead wrote Psychologist B an educative letter, urging that in the future he express himself in more temperate, less accusatory language, and consider contemporary reading on a subject before issuing public statements expressing sharp differences of opinion.*

(Cross-reference to Principle 7.g., under which psychologists are to seek informal solutions to minor misconduct apparently due to a psychologist's lack of knowledge.)

Principle 2.d.

Psychologists recognize differences among people, such as those that may be associated with age, sex, socioeconomic, and ethnic backgrounds. When necessary, they obtain training, experience, or counsel to assure competent service or research relating to such persons.

Case 2.d.1

Mrs. L charged Psychologist M with violation of Section 2.d. for alleged insensitivity to her religious background. A devout Roman Catholic, she was greatly offended by his suggestion during the course of therapy that she might consider the use of birth control. Her family physician had referred the complainant to Psychologist M because one of her children had developed a severe sleep disturbance. She complained to the Ethics Committee that she had sought help from Psychologist M for her child and had no interest in discussing her personal affairs. She contended that her family planning practices were not relevant to the problem at hand.

Psychologist M, a therapist employed by a community mental health center, replied to the Ethics Committee's inquiry that he had been aware of Mrs. L's religion but decided to broach the subject of birth control with her for several reasons. He felt that Mrs. L's anxiety states were in part responsible for her child's sleep disturbances and that her symptoms suggested severe sexual deprivation and frustration, possibly a result of Mr. and Mrs. L's decision to have no more children. Psychologist M said that he saw the situation as a dilemma and had consulted with his supervisor, who had many years of experience in the community, where strict devotion to Roman Catholic tenets was characteristic. The supervisor had seen cases in which sexual abstinence produced family stress and agreed that Psychologist M should seek an opportunity to broach the subject of birth control. He approached the birth control matter gently and did not "suggest" that Mrs. L use birth control, only that she consider doing so. He further stated that he recognized and regretted that Mrs. L had terminated treatment because of this issue. She had allowed her child, however, to continue in treatment at the clinic.

Adjudication: *The Ethics Committee decided that Psychologist M had been sensitive to Mrs. L's religious convictions, in that he had recognized the dilemma her beliefs presented in view of his evaluation of her symptoms and had sought consultation. It therefore found that he had not violated Prin-*

ciple 2.d. of the Ethical Principles *as charged and closed the case.*

Case 2.d.2

The director of a community health center in a Black Haitian community charged Psychologist S with violation of Principle 2.d. A social psychologist, S was investigating the presence of voodoo beliefs and practices, including spiritual healing, among members of the community. Citing complaints he had received, the director charged Psychologist S with employing an interview methodology that was insensitive and ignorant of the community's cultural traditions. He stated further that the interviewers employed by the psychologist conducted themselves in an insulting manner.

Psychologist S replied to the Ethics Committee's inquiry that the subject of the director's complaint was a pilot project terminated several months previously. She felt well qualified to conduct such research because she had spent several years in Haiti as a graduate student and had done her doctoral dissertation on spiritual healing. Furthermore, she spoke French and Patois and felt sensitive to the cultural differences. She trained her graduate students for 2 weeks before sending them into the community; however, she had concluded in retrospect that this was inadequate preparation.

Psychologist S explained that community people had complained about several student interviewers but observed that the center director had not deemed any methodological aspects of the study inappropriate. She concluded that a political issue was the primary source of the project's difficulties: She began the investigation without consulting the community center, the locus of the neighborhood council and other community programs. Psychologist S offered to write a letter apologizing to the director for any offense that she or her students might have caused people who were interviewed, promising to consult with the director before deciding to undertake a full-scale investigation.

Adjudication: *The Ethics Committee was divided initially as to whether to find sufficient evidence to sustain a violation of Principle 2.d. Some committee members assessed the psychologist's actions as poor political judgment rather than cultural insensitivity. The Committee finally reached a consen-*

sus that Psychologist S had not adequately anticipated the consequences of cultural differences between her graduate students and the community in which they would be working. However, her recognition of her misjudgment, her decision to terminate the project, and her willingness to write a letter of apology satisfied the Committee that the situation would be sufficiently rectified, and that no further action would be constructive. The Committee closed the case with an educative letter to Psychologist S stating that, in the future, she must take greater care to select, train, and assess the competence of research assistants employed to work with sensitive social issues and culturally diverse populations. Lastly, the Committee advised that she be more sensitive to the political as well as the social dignity of the population under study.

(Cross-reference to General Principle 9, which cautions psychologists to carry out research with human participants with respect and concern for their dignity and welfare; and to General Principle 1, which requires that, in providing services, psychologists maintain the highest standards of their profession. They accept responsibility for the consequences of their acts and make every effort to ensure that their services are used appropriately.)

Principle 2.e.

Psychologists responsible for decisions involving individuals or policies based on test results have an understanding of psychological or educational measurement, validation problems, and test research.

Case 2.e.1

A candidate for a state civil service position as a prison guard complained to the Ethics Committee that he had been denied the job on the basis of an hour-long test administered to him by Psychologist R, a clinical psychologist and consultant to the corrections department. He scored among the top 25 candidates on the civil service exam and thought he had done well in the interviews, but the candidate understood that he had "failed" the ink blot test administered and apparently interpreted by Psychologist R. He wrote to the Committee that he had questioned Psychologist R concerning the test's relevance to his performance on the job and asked for an opportunity to retake the test. The complainant claimed that Psychologist R refused either to respond to his question about the test's predictive validity or to allow him to retake the test.

Upon receipt of the complaint, the Committee was concerned that Psychologist R might have violated the *Ethical Principles* by using a projective technique of questionable validity in predicting a person's ability to handle the job of prison guard. The Committee charged the psychologist with a potential violation of Principle 2.e. and requested her response to the allegations.

Psychologist R replied that she fully recognized that the Rorschach test is not independently a valid predictor of job success. The corrections department had developed a composite personality picture of the candidate by combining the results of a paper-and-pencil personality inventory, an in-depth interview, and a specific type of Rorschach personality factor analysis. She indicated that her job was to provide a description of candidates' personalities based on the research literature. Corrections department personnel made the hiring decisions, in which Psychologist R was not personally involved. She claimed to have written papers on the limitations of this approach and encouraged the corrections department to develop data on prison guards that could validate the selection criteria. In conclusion, she indicated that the complainant was not rejected on the basis of the Rorschach results, but that departmental confidentiality regulations prevented her giving the Committee more specific information.

Adjudication: *Psychologist R's response quieted the Ethics Committee's concerns as to her role in the selection process; the members found no indication that she knowingly allowed the corrections department to misuse test results. The case was closed on the basis of insufficient evidence to support a finding of an ethical violation.*

> (Cross-reference to Principle 6.b., which states
> that when a psychologist agrees to provide
> services to a client at the request of a third
> party, the psychologist assumes the
> responsibility of clarifying the nature of the
> relationships to all parties concerned; and to

Principle 8.a., which requires that in using assessment techniques, psychologists respect the right of clients to have full explanation of the nature and purpose of the techniques in language the clients can understand, unless an explicit exception to this right has been agreed upon in advance. When the explanations are to be provided by others, psychologists establish procedures for ensuring the adequacy of these explanations.)

Case 2.e.2

A client complained to the Ethics Committee that Psychologist T, his therapist, had informed him that he had severe personality problems. The therapist's assessment was based on the evidence of a doodle the client drew during a session. This episode and similar statements by Psychologist T caused the client to lose confidence in her and terminate therapy. Upset by her diagnosis, which seemed to him without basis, the client questioned how one drawing could justify such an interpretation and charged the psychologist with misuse of testing information.

Psychologist T replied to the Committee's inquiry that the patient's behavior was indeed disturbed and that testing had confirmed this assessment. The Committee requested a copy of the personality test and received a three-sentence "blind" opinion from an art therapist. He had never seen the patient, commented very generally about the drawing, and indicated that certain elements "could suggest deep pathology."

Adjudication: *The Ethics Committee found Psychologist T in violation of Principle 2.e. for an abysmal lack of understanding of the reliability and validity of test procedures and test interpretation. She was censured with the stipulation that she enter a year-long course in personality assessment and refrain in the future from making such comments to her clients based upon this kind of information. The Committee also stipulated that she receive supervision in the use and interpretation of assessment techniques. After Psychologist T accepted the censure and completed the course as required, the case was closed.*

Principle 2.f.

Psychologists recognize that personal problems and conflicts may interfere with professional effectiveness. Accordingly, they refrain from undertaking any activity in which their personal problems are likely to lead to inadequate performance or harm to a client, colleague, student, or research participant. If engaged in such activity when they become aware of their personal problems, they seek competent professional assistance to determine whether they should suspend, terminate, or limit the scope of their professional and/or scientific activities.

Case 2.f.1

A woman charged that, during her second year of treatment, Psychologist L had begun to hug and kiss her before and after each session. A few weeks later he began fondling her in a manner that was physically affectionate and somewhat sexual. This behavior so upset the client that she withdrew from treatment and found a female therapist. She was now very angry, having spent a year of time and money trying to recover from the effects of the experience. Psychologist L was once married, but the client had learned through a newspaper notice that he and his wife had divorced. She realized in retrospect that Psychologist L must have been going through the divorce and in need of physical affection when he initiated the physical contact between them. Although sympathetic with his pain as a result of the divorce, she was angry that he had exploited her because of his personal problems and concerned that he might do the same with other women clients.

When notified of the charges against him and asked to respond by the Ethics Committee, Psychologist L admitted to the behavior and corroborated the complainant's statements that he had experienced considerable personal strain because his wife had terminated their 10-year marriage by leaving him for another man. He said that he was devastated by the situation and drawn to the complainant for affection because of her physical similarity to his wife. He claimed that she was the only client with whom he had had physical contact.

Adjudication: *The Committee found Psychologist L guilty of violating Principles 2.f. and 6.a. of the* Ethical Principles. *In lieu of dropping him from membership, the Committee*

censured him and required that his work with women clients
be carefully supervised by another psychologist, to be mutually
agreed upon between Psychologist L and the Committee. The
Committee required the supervisor to submit progress reports
at 3-month intervals. The supervision would continue until
the Committee received a report from his supervisor that he
was able to handle countertransference issues and to practice
without supervision.

(Cross-reference to Principle 6.a., which
prohibits sexual intimacies with clients and
exploitation of clients' trust, and Principle
7.d., which prohibits sexual harassment.)

Case 2.f.2

A former research assistant charged Psychologist D, principal
investigator for a major research project, with falsely accusing
and subsequently firing the complainant for failure to perform
his work assignments. The complainant claimed that Psychologist D had an alcohol problem so serious that he was
inebriated on the job and frequently forgot instructions he had
issued the day before. The complainant also alleged that his
supervisor had become so irrational in his behavior as to jeopardize the research project. The research assistant concluded
that he had been unfairly fired and that Psychologist D should
be prevented from continuing his tenure as principal investigator for the sake of others employed on the project, whose
dissertations depended on the timely and proper completion
of the research.

The Ethics Committee's initial letter to Psychologist D was
not answered. Psychologist D's secretary, however, replied on
his behalf to the second letter. She indicated that he was in
the hospital and would reply to the charges upon his recovery,
which was expected in a month. Several weeks later, during
which time the Committee made contingency plans to contact
the department head, Psychologist D responded and threw
himself on the mercy of the Committee. He admitted to a
drinking problem. Although he had recognized in himself the
onset of organic symptoms, he had been unable either to control his drinking or seek professional help. He had eventually
had an automobile accident while intoxicated, in·which he
wrecked his car and hurt himself but fortunately injured no

one else. His month in the hospital forced him to stop drinking, and now that he was released and mending, he felt that he could abstain from drinking and rectify the mistake he had made. He had, in fact, initiated the reinstatement of the complainant and submitted a copy of his correspondence with the department head to that effect.

Adjudication: *The Committee found Psychologist D in violation of Principle 2.f. for permitting his personal problems to lead to inadequate professional performance. He was censured with the stipulation that he enroll in a monitored treatment program for his alcoholism and furnish the Committee with a plan for the appropriate supervision of his professional activities. He accepted the censure and complied with the stipulation. The case was closed.*

PRINCIPLE 3   MORAL AND LEGAL STANDARDS

General Principle: Psychologists' moral and ethical standards of behavior are a personal matter to the same degree as they are for any other citizen, except as these may compromise the fulfillment of their professional responsibilities or reduce the public trust in psychology and psychologists. Regarding their own behavior, psychologists are sensitive to prevailing community standards and to the possible impact that conformity to or deviation from these standards may have upon the quality of their performance as psychologists. Psychologists are also aware of the possible impact of their public behavior upon the ability of colleagues to perform their professional duties.

CASE 3.GP.1

An attorney engaged the services of Psychologist L to bolster the defense of her client, a 17-year-old boy accused of sexually molesting a much younger boy. The accused teenager's upbringing was extremely disturbed, he himself having been abused physically and sexually as a young child. The defense attorney asked Psychologist L to testify to the often devastating impact that early abuse may have on a child's development, in the hope that the presiding judge would order the boy to receive psychological services rather than sentence him to incarceration.

Psychologist L appeared at the stipulated time to testify but in an obviously inebriated condition. The shocked attorney was unable to obtain a postponement, so the psychologist was called to the stand. Although he managed to stumble through his testimony, his condition was apparent to all in the courtroom, as he visibly swayed and staggered leaving the witness stand. Later the judge in the case cautioned the jury to disregard Psychologist L's testimony, on the grounds that his condition invalidated his oath.

The defense attorney filed a complaint with the Ethics Committee, pointing out the damage done to her client and to the image of psychologists within the local legal community. When the Ethics Committee contacted Psychologist L, he replied that he was deeply remorseful and pained by what had occurred. He had become so anxious about his first court appearance that he had taken a drink to calm himself down and, unaccustomed to hard liquor, had utterly misjudged the effect it would have. He asked the Committee to forgive his mistake, observing that it was a first offense and would never occur again.

Adjudication: *The Ethics Committee found that Psychologist L had committed a serious breach of General Principle 3, behaving publicly in a way likely to reduce public trust in psychology and to reflect poorly on other psychologists. The Committee reprimanded Psychologist L, placed him on 3 years' probation, and ordered that he not take on any forensic cases.*

CASE 3.GP.2

In a highly publicized case, Psychologist W, a political appointee and highly visible executive in a presidential administration, was arrested and convicted of aiding and abetting prostitution by assisting a young female colleague to place ads in a local newspaper under the guise of legitimate sex therapy. In exchange for a lenient sentence, the young woman provided information that led the local police to arrest Psychologist W, who upon his subsequent conviction was sentenced to several months in jail and lost his state license to practice.

A local psychologist who had read about the arrest and conviction in the newspaper brought the matter to the attention of the Ethics Committee. The Committee brought formal charges *sua sponte* (on its own motion) under General Principle 3 and contacted Psychologist W, asking him to show cause why he should not be expelled from the Association.

The psychologist responded that he had fallen in love with the young woman, who then threatened him with revealing their relationship to the press unless he assisted her with these ads. He stated that he personally found the ads distasteful but felt he had no alternative but to submit them to the newspaper.

Adjudication: *The Committee voted to recommend to the Board of Directors that Psychologist W be dropped from membership for violating General Principle 3; he appealed and requested a Board of Directors' hearing. After the hearing, the panel recommended that he be allowed to resign with the* *stipulation that he not reapply for 5 years and that the membership be notified of this action. Upon receipt of the resignation, the case was closed and the psychologist listed in the annual notice to the membership as having had his membership terminated by stipulated resignation.*

Principle 3.a.

As teachers, psychologists are aware of the fact that their personal values may affect the selection and presentation of instructional materials. When dealing with topics that may give offense, they recognize and respect the diverse attitudes that students may have toward such materials.

Case 3.a.1

An intern wrote to the Ethics Committee complaining that a psychologist had used extremely disturbing videotapes that included graphic descriptions of heinous acts, in conjunction with a nontraditional therapy demonstration. The intern alleged that the behavior shown on the tapes made him ill and violated basic moral standards. He questioned the propriety of using such tapes in therapy or teaching. He further indicated that he had written to the psychologist expressing his concerns but was not satisfied with the reply.

In response to a letter of inquiry from the Ethics Committee, the psychologist wrote a detailed account of the incident, noting that she had invited the intern to discuss his negative feelings more fully, but the intern had refused the invitation. The psychologist outlined safeguards previously established for the demonstration, including (a) a brief description of the tapes and their possible impact, which preceded the showing; (b) the fact that interns were permitted, without penalty, to decline to observe the tapes; and (c) the institution of an extensive debriefing following the demonstration.

The psychologist also set aside time after each viewing of the tape to discuss ethical and other implications and offered to take additional safeguards in the future. She also noted that the tape was not used in therapy as the complainant had alleged; rather, the tape was a demonstration of bad professional practice.

Adjudication: *The Committee was satisfied with the response and did not open a formal case.*

Case 3.a.2

An undergraduate student enrolled in an abnormal psychology course at a large university. Early in the semester the professor gave a lecture that dealt in part with the onset of psychotic symptoms during acute stages of alcoholism. As an aside she told the story of a well-known university president (whom she identified by name) who had suffered from alcoholism for many years, yet managed to control his behavior sufficiently to sustain a successful career. However, by his mid-forties the disease had progressed to the point that he became unable to perform his university duties. After a complete breakdown, during which he suffered hallucinations and violent episodes, he was able to abstain from alcohol and return to work, although his career and health were irreparably damaged.

The student was shocked that this tragic story should have been told to a lecture class of 300 students, revealing the secrets of a person who was still living and struggling to overcome his past. The student had an alcoholic individual in her immediate family and felt very sensitive to the impact of the disease. She felt that the professor had engaged in idle and destructive gossip. The student contacted the APA Ethics Office and subsequently decided to file a complaint.

The professor, contacted by the Ethics Committee, explained that she had studied with the university president of whom she had spoken to the class. The story she had told was essentially the same story the former president had told his own graduate students, and she had passed it along to her class for the same educational purpose: to provide a personal illustration of the serious consequences of acute alcoholism. The professor was deeply apologetic that the story had distressed the student, but she had intended it to serve as a case study, a factual incident relevant to course material.

Adjudication: *The Ethics Committee did not find a violation of Principle 3.a., because the professor had not intended to show disrespect for the student's attitudes or feelings. However, the Committee admonished the professor to use more discretion in the future in revealing such intimate secrets of another's life.*

Principle 3.b.

As employees or employers, psychologists do not engage in or condone practices that are inhumane or that result in illegal or unjustifiable actions. Such practices include, but are not limited to, those based on considerations of race, handicap, age, gender, sexual preference, religion, or national origin in hiring, promotion, or training.

Case 3.b.1

The president of a major land-grant university, Psychologist E, refused to approve the promotion of Dr. W, a female geologist, to associate professor, despite positive recommendations from Dr. W's department and from the faculty senate committee. However, in the same round of personnel decisions, he approved the promotion of Dr. P, a male chemist, to associate professor. Dr. P's record of scholarship and professional recognition in chemistry was comparable with Dr. W's accomplishments in geology.

At the suggestion of a colleague in the university's psychology department, Dr. W submitted a complaint to the Ethics Committee. Psychologist E responded—after a second communication from the Ethics Office—that the Ethics Committee had no jurisdiction over the situation because it concerned his work as a university president, not as a psychologist. He insisted that there were major distinctions between the qualifications of Dr. W and Dr. P, but that he was not free to discuss the details of university personnel decisions with those outside the process.

Adjudication: *The Ethics Committee found Psychologist E in violation of the Preamble to the* Ethical Principles. *There was also considerable evidence that the personnel decision concerning Dr. W was colored by sexual preference, a violation of Principle 3.b. However, Psychologist E had unmistakably violated the ethics code by denying the Committee's jurisdiction over his behavior, a role clearly stated in the Preamble as a condition of membership in APA. The Committee censured him.*

(Cross-reference to the Preamble to the *Ethical Principles*, which sets forth the psychologist's

obligation to cooperate with the APA Ethics
Committee.)

Case 3.b.2

A social worker hired by an inner city mental health clinic
began to realize after less than a year on the job that her
colleagues were padding the records they kept on hours spent
with clients in therapy sessions, apparently in order to collect
higher insurance reimbursements. The practice was so wide-
spread that the social worker soon came to believe that the
clinic director, Psychologist M, must be aware of it. However,
she made an appointment to see the director and informed him
that it was her moral obligation to make this practice publicly
known if it were not immediately stopped. The next day the
social worker received 2-weeks' notice to quit her position and
either leave the clinic or accept another position at much lower
pay with sharply diminished responsibilities.

The social worker filed a complaint against Psychologist M
with the Ethics Committee. Upon response to the Committee's inquiry, Psychologist M responded that the social worker
had proved to be an unsatisfactory employee. He alleged that
her supervisor had serious problems with her treatment of
clients, that she was uncooperative with other staff members,
and that she had a recurrent lateness problem. Informed of
these counter allegations, the social worker was able to present
an excellent 6-month evaluation from her supervisor and from
the social worker who supervised her internship. She challenged Psychologist M to prove the allegations of lateness. He
did not respond.

Adjudication: *The Ethics Committee censured Psychologist
M for violation of Principle 3.b., finding ample evidence that
he had threatened the social worker with firing or demotion
in an attempt to silence her effort to draw attention to the
blatantly fraudulent activity going on at the clinic. The issue
of insurance fraud was not, however, the basis of the censure
and was not at issue in this adjudication.*

Principle 3.c.

In their professional roles, psychologists avoid any action that
will violate or diminish the legal and civil rights of clients or
of others who may be affected by their actions.

Case 3.c.1

The state prison hired Psychologist G to work in the facility's newly organized unit for sex offenders. Psychologist G was a trained clinical psychologist who also held strong religious convictions concerning sexual morality, based on the code of the small sect to which she had converted while in training. In working with inmates she was often overheard to encourage them to pray to God to cleanse themselves of their evil. She was particularly vehement with homosexual inmates, exhorting individuals to "get out their devil."

An inmate complained to the prison warden, who investigated and found the situation to be as alleged. He fired Psychologist G and submitted a complaint about her behavior to the Ethics Committee. Psychologist G was minimally responsive to the inquiries from the Committee.

Adjudication: *The Ethics Committee found overwhelming evidence of Psychologist G's violation of Principle 3.c. On a number of occasions she had approached her clients as if their difficulty were a religious rather than a sexual issue. The Committee debated at length whether to censure or to vote for a stipulated resignation in this case. Ultimately, committee members agreed to censure Psychologist G and require that any practice she undertake be supervised by a psychologist of the Committee's choosing, that she take a course in the ethical practice of psychology, and that she go into treatment herself with a therapist of the Committee's choosing.*

Case 3.c.2

Psychologist R was employed by a satellite community mental health agency in a remote section of Montana. The agency was located in a prosperous town but clients were drawn from as far as 100 miles away, because R was the only licensed psychologist within that geographical radius. The population within the region included a community of Native Americans who had access to no other mental health professionals. However, when approached by potential clients from that community, Psychologist R simply refused to see them, saying only that he preferred not to work with Native Americans.

A visiting nurse who frequently attended patients in the Native American community heard about one such episode and questioned Psychologist R. She was especially surprised because she had understood that his clinical internship had been served with a Native American population in the southwestern United States. He replied that his internship had nothing to do with it; he simply preferred not to work with these people and added that his clients were none of her concern.

The nurse submitted a complaint to the Ethics Committee. Psychologist R replied to the Committee's inquiry he considered himself free to accept only clients with whom he wished to work, because he felt that to do so would maximize his effectiveness and make the best use of his time.

Adjudication: *The Committee found Psychologist R to have violated the civil rights of Native Americans and therefore committed a breach of Principle 3.c. His arbitrary refusal to work with this ethnic community, despite his having appropriate training, deprived an entire population of the only source of psychological services accessible to their community. The Ethics Committee censured Psychologist R and ordered him to cease and desist. He appealed, but the Board of Directors upheld the censure.*

Principle 3.d.

As practitioners and researchers, psychologists act in accord with Association standards and guidelines related to practice and to the conduct of research with human beings and animals. In the ordinary course of events, psychologists adhere to relevant governmental laws and institutional regulations. When federal, state, provincial, organizational, or institutional laws, regulations, or practices are in conflict with Association standards and guidelines, psychologists make known their commitment to Association standards and guidelines and, wherever possible, work toward a resolution of the conflict. Both practitioners and researchers are concerned with the development of such legal and quasi-legal regulations as best serve the public interest, and they work toward changing existing regulations that are not beneficial to the public interest.

Case 3.d.1

A psychologist was employed by a mental health clinic to do individual and group therapy with the clinic's outpatients. The agency director, a psychiatrist, established a new policy that randomly selected treatment reports would be presented to the weekly staff meetings, as a training exercise, and as a way to ensure quality control. Personally identifiable information was included in these reports. The meetings were customarily attended by business and clerical staff as well as by mental health professionals.

The psychologist wrote to the Ethics Committee to ask its opinion—and possibly its assistance—for she was concerned that the new policy might violate the *Ethical Principles*. The Ethics Committee concurred with the psychologist's apprehensions and sent her a strongly worded letter to the effect that the new policy was an abridgment of confidentiality under Principle 5, and would therefore place her in the position of violating her professional code of ethics—a breach of Principle 3.d. as well—were she to carry out the policy mandated by her employer.

The psychologist took the Committee's letter to the agency director and discussed the untenable situation in which she had been placed. Consequently, the director agreed to discontinue the new policy.

(Cross-reference to Principle 5, which pertains to abridgement of confidentiality.)

Case 3.d.2

Having completed an internship, Psychologist E obtained her Ph.D. in counseling psychology and immediately set up a freestanding private practice. She had not yet obtained a license to practice from the state. Discovering this, another psychologist in the area filed a complaint with the Ethics Committee against Psychologist E.

Psychologist E quickly responded to the Committee's inquiry that she was not in violation of the *Ethical Principles* because she considered herself to be in the practice of "psychotherapy" rather than "psychology." However, the complainant supplied the Committee with copies of Psychologist E's letterhead and business cards on which she clearly identified herself as a practitioner of psychology.

Adjudication: *The Ethics Committee found Psychologist E in violation of Principle 3.d. for failing to meet her state's* *licensing requirement for practice. Whether she had identified herself as a psychologist or a psychotherapist was in fact irrelevant to the finding of a violation. The Committee reprimanded Psychologist E and ordered her to cease and desist presenting herself as either a psychologist or a psychotherapist. It also notified the state licensing board for psychology.*

PRINCIPLE 4 **PUBLIC STATEMENTS**

General Principle: Public statements, announcements of services, advertising, and promotional activities of psychologists serve the purpose of helping the public make informed judgments and choices. Psychologists represent accurately and objectively their professional qualifications, affiliations, and functions, as well as those of the institutions or organizations with which they or the statements may be associated. In public statements providing psychological information or professional opinions or providing information about the availability of psychological products, publications, and services, psychologists base their statements on scientifically acceptable psychological findings and techniques with full recognition of the limits and uncertainties of such evidence.

CASE 4.GP

Psychologist T advertised himself as an expert in neuropsychology. He had listed neuropsychology as one of his specialties in notices published in the yellow pages and in two local newspapers. He also had business cards and stationery printed that gave his professional title as "clinical and neuropsychologist." A colleague, Psychologist V, became suspicious because of a diagnostic report she happened to see on a client of Psychologist T's, who had been briefly hospitalized. The report was of such low quality in Psychologist V's judgment that she asked Psychologist T directly what kind of training he had to practice neuropsychology. When she was refused an answer, Psychologist V submitted a complaint to the Ethics Committee.

Psychologist T responded to the Ethics Committee's inquiry that he had attended two 1-day workshops and done substantial independent reading on neuropsychology. The Committee then asked for evidence of supervised training, and Psychologist T was unable to furnish any.

Adjudication: *The Ethics Committee censured Psychologist T and mandated that he cease and desist either advertising himself as a neuropsychologist or engaging in the practice of neuropsychology.*

(Cross-reference to General Principle 2, which pertains to the psychologist's responsibility to practice only in areas for which one is qualified by training and experience.)

Principle 4.a.

When announcing or advertising professional services, psychologists may list the following information to describe the provider and services provided: name, highest relevant academic degree earned from a regionally accredited institution, date, type, and level of certification or licensure, diplomate status, APA membership status, address, telephone number, office hours, a brief listing of the type of psychological services offered, an appropriate presentation of fee information, foreign languages spoken, and policy with regard to third-party payments. Additional relevant or important consumer information may be included if not prohibited by other sections of these *Ethical Principles.*

Case 4.a.

Psychologist X, who had recently moved to a new community, decided to advertise in order to establish a private practice. Before doing so, however, she wrote to the Ethics Committee, inquiring as to whether the following advertisement met APA guidelines:

I. M. PSYCHOLOGIST, Ph.D.

Diplomate in Clinical Psychology

American Board of Professional Psychology

Treatment for emotional troubles (Psychotherapy)

Marriage problems consultations

Sexual difficulties

Biofeedback Relaxation Training
(for tensions, irritability, headaches,
sleep problems, etc.)

Behavior and school problems of
children, teenagers

Personality studies and I.Q. determination
Sliding scale fees. First half-hour of
consultation free. Eligible for insurance coverage,
if client has it.

0000 Local Neighborhood Drive, Anywhere, State
By appointment.   Telephone 000-0000

Opinion: The Ethics Committee reviewed the advertisement and agreed that it was appropriately written but expressed concern with the statement "First half-hour of consultation free." The potential for a "foot-in-the-door" situation would be created, whether in reality or only in the client's mind. The client might feel obligated to return because of receiving a free service or feel otherwise indebted to the psychologist. Finally, many clients make a major emotional investment during a first session and might unwittingly commit themselves to a longer term relationship than they would have otherwise. The Committee preferred, if necessary, that the psychologist make the last half-hour free, as opposed to the first half-hour. It was hoped this step would eliminate the possible foot-in-the-door problem. However, the ad was seen as consistent with the ethical code. The APA does encourage *pro bono* services and requires prior disclosure of fees (Principle 6.d.). But, in any event, the ethical code is appropriately silent concerning the actual amount of fees charged.

Principle 4.b.

In announcing or advertising the availability of psychological products, publications, or services, psychologists do not present their affiliation with any organization in a manner that falsely implies sponsorship or certification by that organization. In particular and for example, psychologists do not state APA membership or fellow status in a way to suggest that such status implies specialized professional competence or qualifications. Public statements include, but are not limited to, communication by means of periodical, book, list, directory, television, radio, or motion picture. They do not contain (i) a false, fraudulent, misleading, deceptive, or unfair statement; (ii) a misinterpretation of fact or a statement likely to mislead or deceive because in context it makes only a partial disclosure of relevant facts; (iii) a testimonial from a patient regarding the quality of a psychologist's services or products; (iv) a statement intended or likely to create false or unjustified expectations of favorable results; (v) a statement implying unusual, unique, or one-of-a-kind abilities; (vi) a statement intended or likely to appeal to a client's fears, anxieties, or emotions concerning the possible results of failure to obtain the offered services; (vii) a statement concerning the comparative desirability of offered services; (viii) a statement of direct solicitation of individual clients.

Case 4.b.

A psychologist advertised pain control as one of the services he provided to clients. His advertisements explained in some detail the techniques he employed to help control pain and included a statement to the effect that the American Psychological Association had endorsed his approach. A social worker who noticed his advertisement was curious about the endorsement of a particular therapeutic method by a professional organization and asked the psychologist for the details of the APA's endorsement. When he refused to provide these, she became suspicious and brought an ethics charge against the psychologist.

The Ethics Committee contacted the psychologist and asked him to substantiate the claim of an endorsement. He replied that on several occasions he had led workshops on pain control under the sponsorship of a private clinic that had become an "approved sponsor" through the APA Continuing Education sponsor approval system. Because his workshops were held under these auspices, he had assumed that his workshop and the method he taught had the implied endorsement of the APA.

Adjudication: *The Ethics Committee cautioned the psychologist that sponsorship by an APA-approved sponsor is absolutely not equivalent to endorsement by the APA. The Committee ordered him to cease and desist immediately. Because no client had been harmed and no consumer had complained, the Committee took no further action other than to tell the psychologist to remove all statements concerning APA endorsement from his advertising. The psychologist agreed to do so.*

Principle 4.c.

Psychologists do not compensate or give anything of value to a representative of the press, radio, television, or other communication medium in anticipation of or in return for professional publicity in a news item. A paid advertisement must be identified as such, unless it is apparent from the context that it is a paid advertisement. If communicated to the public by use of radio or television, an advertisement is prerecorded and approved for broadcast by the psychologist, and a recording of the actual transmission is retained by the psychologist.

Case 4.c.

Psychologist Z had a well-established private practice in a major midwest city. As the city experienced a population boom, other therapists began to move into the area and challenge Psychologist Z's monopoly on psychotherapy in the private sector. To obtain publicity for his practice, Psychologist Z offered a local news anchor $250 to arrange for the station's news team to film a television special about him. When the anchor refused, Psychologist Z tried the same approach with a news reporter from the competing station, offering her $400. When she also turned him down, he pursued the local affiliate for a cable station. One of the reporters was so angered by the episode that she contacted the state psychological association and then filed a complaint with the state ethics committee.

Because of the allegation that Psychologist Z had offered reporters substantial sums of money, the case was first forwarded to the local district attorney. He prosecuted and obtained a conviction. Psychologist Z had denied the charge against him and refused to cooperate in any way with the investigating authorities. As a result of his conviction on the felony charge and his subsequent refusal to cooperate with the state ethics committee, the committee expelled him from the state psychological association.

The APA Ethics Committee *sua sponte* (on its own motion) brought charges against Psychologist Z and asked him to show cause why he should not be dropped from the APA. Psychologist Z refused to submit to the Committee's inquiries on the grounds that he had been persecuted unjustly by the local press and the district attorney and would not subject himself to further humiliation and abuse. Moreover, he accused the Ethics Committee of overstepping the bounds of its authority by meddling in a matter under the jurisdiction of the courts.

Adjudication: *The Committee found Psychologist Z in violation of Principle 4.c. and dropped him from membership in the Association. The Committee found that he had flagrantly violated both legal and ethical standards and furthermore was so uncooperative in the matter that he had violated the Preamble to the* Ethical Principles *as well.*

(Cross-reference to the Preamble to the *Ethical Principles,* which sets forth the psychologist's obligation to cooperate with the APA Ethics Committee and the state association ethics committees.)

Principle 4.d.

Announcements or advertisements of "personal growth groups," clinics, and agencies give a clear statement of purpose and a clear description of the experiences to be provided. The education, training, and experience of the staff members are appropriately specified.

Case 4.d.

A woman signed up for a weekend encounter group to be led by Psychologist X at the psychologist's home in a secluded resort area. The woman's expectations for the session were based on a printed brochure and several flyers distributed by Psychologist X a month previously at a local health fair. The brochure advertised the encounter as conducive to personal growth and enlightenment and noted that "body-work" was part of the weekend's activity, citing as examples daily hatha yoga exercise and workouts in the Olympic-size swimming pool.

However, soon after the woman arrived for the encounter group, she discovered that she was expected to disrobe entirely for the pool session. As she was debating what to do, she learned from another attendee, a participant in previous encounter groups led by Psychologist X, that the swim session would be followed by a massage workshop, also conducted in the nude. Rather than comply with these requirements, she left the group and filed a complaint with the Ethics Committee.

Upon investigation the Ethics Committee did find that the materials the complainant submitted as evidence had mentioned neither nudity nor communal body massage. When queried, Psychologist X explained that she had recently changed her methodology, having become convinced that deep body-work was conducive to the most radical and profound therapeutic change in the context of the group encounter. She was in the process of developing new promotional materials that would describe her philosophy of treatment and explain the rationale for the activities, including nudity and massage.

Adjudication: *The Ethics Committee found Psychologist X in clear violation of Principle 4.d. and reprimanded her, stipulating that she cease and desist conducting groups that involved nudity or massage, unless and until she could provide prospective participants with adequate notice and an explanation of what to expect in the group experience.*

Principle 4.e.

Psychologists associated with the development or promotion of psychological devices, books, or other products offered for commercial sale make reasonable efforts to ensure that announcements and advertisements are presented in a professional, scientifically acceptable, and factually informative manner.

Case 4.e.

Two psychologists claimed in their advertisements that they had achieved a startling breakthrough in developing a new and unique therapeutic technique. They asserted that the treatment provided "profound and surprising" insights into behavior and produced clients who "actually get well," even clients whom other therapists had been unable to help. Promoting themselves as the "George Washington" and "Abraham Lincoln" of a revolutionary new mode of psychotherapy, they appeared on radio and television talk shows and many public seminars on health and self-help. They placed advertisements making the same claims in local newspapers and national circulation magazines. In their public statements and promotional materials they claimed to be "myth busters" and cited glowing testimonials to their work from authors of fictional and nonfictional books that dealt with psychological themes.

In response to the Ethics Committee's inquiry, the pair explained that they had used the new treatment mode in their joint private practice for more than 5 years and were well satisfied by its efficacy. Unable to indicate any research that supported their claims for successful treatment, the psychologists explained that they had thought it more important to get the word out about an effective treatment than to waste time on laboratory exercises that could only at best simulate the therapeutic situation. Moreover, they argued that the hyperbolic tone of their advertisements and appearances was simply the language of public performance and promotion. One could not expect the public to have the patience to try to interpret the monotonous and unnecessarily obscure jargon of the profession.

Adjudication: *It was the consensus of the Ethics Committee that the advertisements used by these psychologists to promote their books and public lectures were neither professional, scientifically acceptable, nor factually informative. Rather, sensational statements and insupportable claims were made, rendering the advertisements classic examples of unprofessional behavior and gross exaggeration and therefore clear violations of Principle 4.e. The Committee reprimanded the psychologists, ordered them to cease using these ads and mandated that they clear future ads with the Committee to ensure that they were not deceptive or misleading.*

Principle 4.f.

Psychologists do not participate for personal gain in commercial announcements or advertisements recommending to the public the purchase or use of proprietary or single-source products or services when that participation is based solely upon their identification as psychologists.

Case 4.f.

A leading industrial/organizational psychologist became well known among the general public after his book on aggression and athletes became a best seller. Psychologist Q appeared on talk shows and was extensively interviewed in the press during the promotion campaign set up by his publisher. His tanned, rugged appearance and irreverent wit made him popular with audiences.

The advertising agency that handled the account of a major tennis equipment manufacturer, taking note of the attractive image the psychologist had so quickly developed, asked him to endorse their product in a series of magazine advertisements. He agreed, and the advertisements appeared in several national circulation magazines, featuring his photograph and identifying him specifically as an industrial/organizational psychologist. The ad quoted him as stating that, as a psychologist, he found that using this tennis equipment had improved his game.

Informed by several APA members that the advertisement had appeared, the Ethics Committee in turn notified the psychologist that he had committed an apparent violation of Principle 4.f. of the *Ethical Principles*. In response, the psychologist pleaded ignorance of this section of the ethics code.

Adjudication: *The Committee was not moved by the psychologist's plea, observing that ignorance of the ethics code, like ignorance of the law, is not an adequate excuse for violating the code. The Committee reprimanded the psychologist and agreed to keep the case open for the 5-year maximum to ensure that the unethical behavior would not be repeated.*

Principle 4.g.

Psychologists present the science of psychology and offer their services, products, and publications fairly and accurately, avoiding misrepresentation through sensationalism, exaggeration, or superficiality. Psychologists are guided by the primary obligation to aid the public in developing informed judgments, opinions, and choices.

Case 4.g.

Two psychologists testified on opposite sides in a court hearing that concerned the degree of brain damage a child had suffered in an automobile accident. Psychologist H gave a deposition that assessed a psychological evaluation previously performed by Psychologist G on the child. In her deposition, Psychologist

H not only stated that the evaluation had been poorly performed, but she couched her criticism in sensationalistic and inflammatory language, accusing Psychologist G of having demonstrated "reprehensible ignorance" of the impact of such injuries on the developing brain. In her testimony she further accused Psychologist G of misusing her professional standing to "harm irreparably" the child's chance of obtaining a settlement that could pay for the necessary years of special education and therapy, and she added that Psychologist G must have been a "paid lackey" in the service of a "miserly" insurance company to behave in such a "criminal fashion."

After reading this deposition, Psychologist G submitted a complaint to the Ethics Committee. In response to the Committee's inquiry, Psychologist H stood by her deposition and insisted that she had been truly shocked by the poor quality of the evaluation performed on the child and was entirely convinced it could only reflect either criminal carelessness or the insurance company's dictates.

Adjudication: *The Committee reviewed the testimony by both psychologists at the court hearing and concluded that Psychologist H could have communicated her concerns about Psychologist G's competence in less inflammatory terms and as such had overstepped the bounds of acceptable professional behavior in her deposition. A more appropriate way for Psychologist H to have expressed her concerns would have been to file a complaint with the Ethics Committee. The Committee mandated that she send a letter of apology to the complainant. When she refused and again stood by her deposition, the Committee persevered, stating that the alternative was a recommendation from the Ethics Committee to the Board of Directors for her expulsion. Psychologist H then grudgingly apologized and the case was closed.*

Principle 4.h.

As teachers, psychologists ensure that statements in catalogs and course outlines are accurate and not misleading, particularly in terms of subject matter to be covered, bases for evaluating progress, and the nature of course experiences. Announcements, brochures, or advertisements describing workshops, seminars, or other educational programs accurately describe the audience for which the program is intended as well as eligibility requirements, educational objectives, and nature of the materials to be covered. These announcements also accurately represent the education, training, and experience of the psychologists presenting the programs and any fees involved.

Case 4.h.

A graduate professor in a clinical psychology program taught a course on group therapy practice. The course summary in the college catalog described it as a review of current theoretical positions concerning group therapy. A graduate student signed up for the course and discovered at the first session that one of the requirements was for him to enter into a therapy group with his classmates, the group to be led by their professor. He protested this arrangement to the professor. She responded that the only way to learn to do group therapy was to go through the experience oneself. She dismissed the failure to mention the requirement in the description as merely an unimportant oversight.

Not mollified, the student decided to press charges with the Ethics Committee, which investigated the matter as a possible violation of both Principle 4.h. and Principle 6.a. When the Committee approached the professor, she gave the members a response similar to her explanation to the student. The course was experiential, she insisted; there was no way to complete the course or to learn group therapy without being in a group oneself. She explained further that the printed course description was in error and soon to be corrected. She added that how a student performed in group therapy had no influence whatsoever on the course grade he or she received.

Adjudication: *The Ethics Committee found clear violations of both Principles 4.h. and 6.a. The Committee censured the psychologist and ordered her to see that all course descriptions in the future accurately reflected the nature of the course. The Committee also ordered her to cease and desist engaging in dual relationships. The Ethics Committee found further that, if the program required a group experience of its clinical graduate students, the experience would have to be clearly spelled out in the program description, and the group leaders would have to be persons not affiliated in any way with the clinical graduate program.*

(Cross-reference to Principle 6.a., which directs psychologists to avoid dual relationships, including treatment of individuals who are also their students.)

Principle 4.i.

Public announcements or advertisements soliciting research participants in which clinical services or other professional services are offered as an inducement make clear the nature of the services as well as the costs and other obligations to be accepted by participants in the research.

Case 4.i.

Psychologist Y advertised in her city's daily newspaper for research subjects to participate in an 18-month study of "Type A" personalities. The advertisement specified her interest in subjects who were "aggressive, hard-driving, ambitious." People who responded to the advertisement were told by Psychologist Y that she would screen all subjects and assess their level of Type A characteristics. She would then place all subjects, she explained, into treatment groups based on either psychotherapy, behavior modification, or control modes of treatment. The purpose of these placements was to train the subjects to become "Type B personalities: assertive, laid back, and successful." The subjects were told that they would not have to pay for the screening but would have to pay for the therapy sessions, in order to simulate the experience of therapy in real life. She indicated that third-party payments might be accepted.

Six months into the project several research subjects became suspicious, realizing that no one was conducting research or appeared to have any plans to do so. Several subjects wrote a joint letter to the Ethics Committee.

In response to the Committee's inquiry, Psychologist Y acknowledged that no research was underway. She explained that originally she had intended to conduct the research study as advertised and still hoped eventually to do so. However, she was currently unable to begin the study because of the demands of treating so many Type A personalities. She further admitted that she had not established a control group.

Adjudication: *The Ethics Committee found that Psychologist Y's advertisements soliciting research subjects were clearly fraudulent, a violation of Principle 4.i. The Committee recommended that she be dropped from membership in APA, and the Board of Directors concurred.*

Principle 4.j.

A psychologist accepts the obligation to correct others who represent the psychologist's professional qualifications, or associations with products or services, in a manner incompatible with these guidelines.

Case 4.j.

A professional private practice center offering psychotherapy and psychological evaluation to the public published a brochure listing several of the staff inaccurately. Some of the errors included listing psychologist Z as a Diplomate in Clinical Psychology when in fact he was not, listing a staff member as a member of APA when in fact he was not, and listing a staff member as "Dr." when in fact she had only a master's degree.

Psychologist Z telephoned the director of the clinic, and on the basis of Principles 4.j. and 7.g., made an inquiry regarding these three discrepancies. The director became agitated and defensive and rebutted the psychologist. She stated that Psychologist Z had applied for an ABPP certificate and she was sure he would get it. Secondly, the director was certain the staff member who had applied for APA membership would receive it. Thirdly, the staff member listed as "Dr." was a candidate for an Ed.D. at an out-of-state institution. All three errors were events imminently anticipated by the director. She then stated that she would not withdraw or modify the brochure unless it became clear that one of the anticipated events would not occur.

Psychologist Z withdrew his affiliation from the private practice center and then registered a written complaint with the Ethics Committee, because the clinic director was also an APA member.

Adjudication: *Upon inquiry by the Committee, the clinic director and the applicant for APA membership became* *enraged, declaring that a mountain had been made out of a molehill. The director attempted to resign her APA membership but this step was blocked by the APA Ethics Office; it is standard operating procedure not to allow a member to resign while under investigation by the Ethics Committee.*

Lacking the director's cooperation, for she refused to withdraw the advertisement, the Ethics Committee referred the case to the Board of Directors, recommending that her membership in APA be dropped for violations of Principle 4.j. and of the Preamble to the ethical code, for failure to cooperate. The Committee also forwarded the case to the state attorney general's office and the board of examiners of psychologists because of probable illegalities in advertising.

(Cross-reference to the Preamble to the *Ethical Principles*, which sets forth the psychologist's obligation to cooperate with the APA Ethics Committee, and to Principle 4.b., which forbids psychologists from making false or misleading public statements about their organizational affiliations.)

Principle 4.k.

Individual diagnostic and therapeutic services are provided only in the context of a professional psychological relationship. When personal advice is given by means of public lectures or demonstrations, newspaper or magazine articles, radio or television programs, mail, or similar media, the psychologist utilizes the most current relevant data and exercises the highest level of professional judgment.

Case 4.k.

An academic psychologist planning to vacation in a popular northeastern resort area inquired of the Ethics Committee whether it would be ethical to set up an "individual diagnostic and therapeutic service" in an area with many vacationing tourists. He explained that he planned to use projective drawing techniques and handwriting analysis, assisted by his own knowledge and skill. He would complete the testing and therapy of each "client" in 15 minutes and conduct each session so that passing tourists could stop and observe. The process would maintain anonymity because the population was so transient that no one really knew anyone. Also the opportunity to observe would educate many passersby.

Opinion: After writing to the psychologist for further clarification, the Ethics Committee determined that the psychologist proposed to operate in the fashion of fortunetellers or psychics, who are often found in a carnival setting. Furthermore, he planned to set up a booth to contain his office and handwriting analysis machine, which although computerized featured a colorful display of lights and noises when in operation. The psychologist was informed that he needed to conform to the licensure law of the state in order to provide diagnostic and therapeutic services and that such services are not to be provided in a carnival atmosphere; when in the public arena, psychologists must use the most current and relevant data and execute the highest level of professional judgment. In summary, what the psychologist had planned was unethical and possibly in violation of the licensure laws of his state. So informed, the psychologist gave up the idea and thanked the Committee.

Principle 4.I.

Products that are described or presented by means of public lectures or demonstrations, newspaper or magazine articles, radio or television programs, or similar media meet the same recognized standards as exist for products used in the context of a professional relationship.

Case 4.I.

It was brought to the attention of the Ethics Committee that an APA member had invented a "self-administered" paper-and-pencil IQ test and marketed it nationwide through several magazines. The advertisement stated that a valid measure of intelligence could be obtained by answering 20 questions. Answers to the questions were to be mailed to the psychologist along with $10.

An Ethics Committee member ordered the test, took it, returned her answers, and received a note from the psychologist stating that her IQ was 130 and "Very superior." The 20 questions were taken verbatim from three well-known and widely used individual intelligence tests. Based on these findings, the Committee opened a case, filing formal *sua sponte* (on its own motion) charges against the psychologist for a possible violation of Principle 4.1. as well as of General Principle 1.

Adjudication: *From the answers to the series of questions asked by the Ethics Committee, it became obvious that the psychologist had never properly standardized or validated the test, nor had she constructed the test in a reasonable and logical, scientific and methodologically sound fashion, based on the body of knowledge already accumulated on the subject of intelligence and intelligence testing. Although brief IQ tests and personality tests have been adequately constructed in the past, such was clearly not the case in this instance. Furthermore, the psychologist had plagiarized the questions on the test and used them without permission.*

The Committee recommended to the APA Board of Directors that the psychologist be dropped from membership for violation of Principle 4.1., and the Board concurred.

(Cross-reference to General Principle 1, which requires psychologists to uphold the highest standards of their profession, and to Principle 8.b., which requires psychologists to utilize established scientific procedures and observe relevant APA standards in developing assessment techniques.)

PRINCIPLE 5   **CONFIDENTIALITY**

General Principle: Psychologists have a primary obligation to respect the confidentiality of information obtained from persons in the course of their work as psychologists. They reveal such information to others only with the consent of the person or the person's legal representative, except in those unusual circumstances in which not to do so would result in clear danger to the person or to others. Where appropriate, psychologists inform their clients of the legal limits of confidentiality.

CASE 5.GP.1

A complaint was lodged against a psychologist in independent practice by one of his psychotherapy clients. The complainant alleged that the psychologist had sent copies of his case notes to the insurance carrier responsible for reimbursing the psychologist, insisted the psychologist had no business revealing such information, and therefore accused him of violating Principle 5 of the *Ethical Principles.*

In response to the Ethics Committee's inquiry, the psychologist pointed out that, when a psychotherapy client wishes to use an insurance carrier for third-party reimbursement, the client must understand that the confidentiality of the therapeutic relationship can be abridged for the purpose of administrative and professional peer review. However, the psychologist had never informed the client of this risk prior to the initiation of therapy, assuming instead that the client "must understand" the situation.

Adjudication: *The Ethics Committee found the psychologist in violation of General Principle 5 of the* Ethical Principles *for failure to inform the client of the legal limits of confidentiality prior to initiating treatment. The Committee reprimanded the psychologist and advised him to develop and implement an adequate informed consent process in the future.*

CASE 5.GP.2

The Ethics Committee received a complaint by an unmarried 17-year-old student against a psychologist employed by a university counseling service. The psychologist had supervised the student's counselor, who was working as a predoctoral intern in the counseling service. The psychologist was an APA member; the intern was not.

The complainant alleged that the supervising psychologist had violated the confidentiality of the client–therapist relationship by informing the student's parents of his suicide threat. The student had refused to seek voluntary hospitalization, which the intern had strongly suggested that he do. The intern informed the supervising psychologist of the suicide threat during a routine supervisory session. The intern was concerned about the risk of an attempt because the student was agitated and depressed and had made a suicide attempt several years previously. The supervisor required the intern to give her the student's name and other identifying data so that she could notify the parents.

Once notified, the parents immediately came to campus and had the student hospitalized. After his brief hospitalization, the student initiated the complaint against the psychologist for breach of confidentiality.

In response to the Ethics Committee's inquiry, the psychologist indicated that her actions were consistent with Principle 5 of the *Ethical Principles*. On the basis of the information she received from the intern, clear danger of harm to the student existed. Because the law in her state allowed immediate relatives to request involuntary hospitalization, and the student had refused voluntary admission, and because the psychologist and the intern did not want to proceed unilaterally, it was necessary and proper to notify the student's parents in order to protect his welfare.

Adjudication: *The Ethics Committee agreed that there was no substantial evidence of a violation of Principle 5. The psychologist was presented with a conflict between the principle of confidentiality, the duty to protect the client's welfare, and the interests of the parents in participating in treatment decisions concerning their dependent minor child. In this case the Committee concurred with the psychologist's reasonable judgment that the possibility of losing the student to suicide* *justified informing the parents and disclosing information about their son's treatment.*

Principle 5.a.

Information obtained in clinical or consulting relationships, or evaluative data concerning children, students, employees, and others, is discussed only for professional purposes and only with persons clearly concerned with the case. Written and oral reports present only data germane to the purposes of the evaluation, and every effort is made to avoid undue invasion of privacy.

Case 5.a.1

A staff member of a social service agency complained that a psychologist on the agency staff frequently discussed—at lunch and other informal gatherings—therapy sessions with his private practice clients. The complainant had suggested several times to the psychologist that his behavior seemed unprofessional, but he had assured her that there was no problem since he never revealed a client's name.

Matters came to a head one day when the complainant realized that the client the psychologist was discussing had worked for the agency. The details the psychologist revealed made it easy to identify the client. The complainant felt that she had tried without success to resolve the matter directly with the psychologist and, therefore, lodged a formal complaint with the Ethics Committee.

In response to the committee's inquiry, the psychologist responded that he was careful never to reveal a client's name in discussing a case. He added that he believed his efforts to seek the advice of his colleagues in informal conversation were ethical and of benefit to his clients.

Adjudication: *The Ethics Committee found the psychologist guilty of violating Principle 5.a. of the* Ethical Principles. *Agency staff members have no legitimate connection to private practice clients. Even if the discussions only involved agency clients, such conversations should never take place in a public or quasi-public setting such as a lunchroom. Even in privacy, only appropriately concerned members of the agency staff should participate. As this case demonstrates, failing to dis-*

close a client's name does not assure anonymity. If a private practitioner wishes to consult another therapist, the psychologist must get the client's permission to do so. Any psychologist working in a supervised setting or with clients using third-party payments should outline to the client at the outset the limits of confidentiality inherent in these relationships as well as the legal limits of confidentiality. The Ethics Committee censured the psychologist, ordered him to desist from such behavior, and informed him that the Committee would be forced to respond more harshly if another violation were reported and confirmed.

Case 5.a.2

Several psychologists wrote to the Ethics Committee to complain about an APA member who had appeared on radio and TV talk shows with a number of her clients, all of whom were well-known stars in the entertainment industry. In the talk show format, the psychologist encouraged her clients, some of whom had terminated treatment and others of whom were still active clients, to talk about their reasons for seeking treatment and their experiences in therapy. The complainants argued that the program clearly violated the psychologist–client confidentiality principle, especially Principle 5.a., because it was not professional, disclosed the identity of clients, and revealed details of treatment.

   In response to the Ethics Committee's inquiry, the psychologist revealed that her clients themselves had suggested this show. She had thoroughly discussed the pros and cons of self-disclosure with them, and all had agreed that the benefits to the general public of their self-disclosure outweighed any risk involved. The psychologist had obtained written informed consent agreements, and all the clients were willing to provide statements to attest to what had transpired.

Adjudication: *On the basis of the information furnished, the Committee decided that there was insufficient evidence to support a charge of ethical violation of Principle 5.a. Although several members felt that the psychologist may not have acted in good taste, they found insufficient evidence to support ethical charges against the psychologist.*

Principle 5.b.

Psychologists who present personal information obtained during the course of professional work in writings, lectures, or other public forums either obtain adequate prior consent to do so or adequately disguise all identifying information.

Case 5.b.1

Psychologist O was a tenured faculty member of the psychology department at a small university. In addition to her teaching duties, Psychologist O worked as a counselor on the staff of the university health services center. Every other year she taught the undergraduate abnormal psychology lecture course, which typically enrolled 100 students or more. To interest her students in the material, Psychologist O often provided hypothetical case studies that illustrated the particular symptom or syndrome about which she was lecturing. During her presentation on love and depression, Psychologist O described a case similar in many particulars to that of a junior psychology major whose affair with a basketball player had publicly dissolved during the previous winter. The student had briefly gone into counseling with Psychologist O after the breakup. In her lecture the psychologist alluded to the young woman's attempted suicide and hospitalization, events not previously public knowledge.

Several students reported this episode to the student, who, furious and distraught, consulted her advisor, Psychologist S. She in turn confronted Psychologist O, who insisted that on those occasions when she did refer to actual events and individuals she did so only after substantially altering the circumstances surrounding the case.

Psychologist S, convinced of the student's grievance, filed a complaint with the Ethics Committee. Upon receipt of the Committee's inquiry, Psychologist O again insisted that she had taken all precautions to disguise any personal information about real cases that she used in her class lectures or any other presentations. When confronted by a letter from her former client to the Ethics Committee, detailing the parallels between Psychologist O's lecture and her real life case, Psychologist O indicated that perhaps she could have disguised the information more effectively.

71

Adjudication: *The Ethics Committee found Psychologist C in violation of Principle 5.b. of the* Ethical Principles *for failing to disguise adequately information obtained during the course of her professional work. The Committee voted to censure.*

Case 5.b.2

Psychologist G conducted a professional evaluation of the accused murderer in a sensational and well-publicized case in which six teenage girls, who vanished over a period of 18 months, were later found stabbed to death in an abandoned waterfront area of the city. The lurid nature of the crimes attracted nationwide publicity, which only increased as allegations of negligence were pressed against the city administration and the police force. In order to construct a psychological diagnostic profile, Psychologist G spent several days with the accused, conducting interviews and psychometric tests. He presented his findings in court with the full consent of the accused.

Six months later, following the sentencing of the now convicted murderer, Psychologist G determined that he would like to write a book about the murderer and the psychology behind the crimes, which he anticipated would be a lucrative undertaking. Psychologist G wrote to the Ethics Committee to inquire whether it would be ethical for him to do so. The convicted murderer had refused permission to publish in a book the results of the psychological evaluation, despite the fact that the information was now considered part of the public domain because it had been admitted in court as evidence.

Opinion: The Ethics Committee responded to Psychologist G that to write the proposed book would be a legal but unethical undertaking. The fact that material has entered the public domain or that there may have been an implied waiver of consent does not free the psychologist from the obligation under Principle 5.b. of the *Ethical Principles* to obtain prior consent before presenting in a public forum personal information acquired through the course of professional work. In this case, the ethics code sets a higher standard of behavior than the law would require. Psychologist G thanked the Committee for its advice and dropped the idea of writing the book.

Principle 5.c.

Psychologists make provisions for maintaining confidentiality in the storage and disposal of records.

Case 5.c.1

One year after terminating therapy with Psychologist V, his former client decided to reenter treatment but selected another psychotherapist in the city to which she had moved. She wrote to Psychologist V to request that all his records of her treatment be sent to her new therapist. He responded by letter that he would try to do so, but that it might take him a few weeks to comply with her request because his office had been burglarized and his records were in complete disarray. Two months later the client's new therapist advised her that he had yet to receive any records or any other communication from Psychologist V. The client again wrote to Psychologist V and this time received no response. After another 2 weeks she placed a long-distance call to Psychologist V. He returned her call and apologized for his intransigence, explaining that her records had in fact disappeared in the burglary, but he had delayed notifying her in the hope that the police would locate them. However, with the passage of so many weeks, he realized that the likelihood of the records ever showing up now seemed dim.

On the advice of her new therapist, the client filed a complaint against Psychologist V with the Ethics Committee. He responded to the Committee that he deeply regretted the loss of his former client's records and admitted that neither his office nor his client records were customarily locked up. He rarely locked his private office because the suite door was locked when none of the professionals were holding office hours. Psychologist V explained that few people in his small town regularly locked their homes or their businesses because crime was so rare. However, this experience had taught him that crime could happen anywhere and from now on he would keep all his records under lock and key.

Adjudication: *The Ethics Committee found Psychologist V in violation of Principle 5.c. The* Ethical Principles *bind psychologists to assure confidentiality in storing and disposing of records; the fact that his client records were stolen from an* *unlocked office demonstrated that Psychologist V had not adequately provided for the care of his records. The Committee reprimanded Psychologist V and sent him a strongly worded educative letter, explaining that good intentions did not excuse his negligence.*

Case 5.c.2

During a session with Psychologist B, a client noticed that a file cabinet in the office appeared to be unlocked. The client demanded to know whether confidential client records were kept in what appeared to be an unlocked cabinet. Psychologist B confirmed that the cabinet contained client records and was kept unlocked but attempted to reassure her client by explaining that the office itself was secure. Within a month, the client abruptly and prematurely terminated therapy, soon thereafter filing a complaint with the Ethics Committee against his former therapist, alleging that client records were not stored in a way to ensure confidentiality.

In response to the Committee's inquiry about this matter, Psychologist B responded that the complaint was the act of an aggrieved individual. She explained that all her client records were stored in the file cabinet in question and in a similar cabinet not noted by the client, both of which were never locked. However, the office in which the cabinets were located was never left unlocked except when she herself was present. The office locks were secure, and the office further safeguarded by an alarm system.

Adjudication: *Persuaded that Psychologist B had taken adequate measures to ensure the confidentiality of her records, the Ethics Committee found no violation of Principle 5.c. and dropped the case.*

Principle 5.d.

When working with minors or other persons who are unable to give voluntary, informed consent, psychologists take special care to protect these persons' best interests.

Case 5.d.1

A school psychologist was conducting research into the effectiveness of the sex education offered by elementary schools. To evaluate these programs she decided it was essential that she interview elementary school children themselves. The psychologist interviewed 30 sixth-graders about their knowledge and feelings on a variety of issues related to sexuality without first obtaining written permission from their parents.

Several parents complained to the school administration; one submitted a formal complaint to the Ethics Committee. The psychologist responded to the Committee's inquiry that she had taken extreme care in preparing the students to be interviewed. She had spoken more than once in classes about her research and why she needed to talk with students, and she had received the oral permission of each student she interviewed. Moreover, she had asked the students to speak ahead of time with their parents so that any of their fears could be allayed by the psychologist in a timely fashion. Receiving no word of any objection from the students' parents, she assumed that all were amenable to the interviews.

Adjudication: *The Ethics Committee found the psychologist in violation of Principle 5.d. for failure to take sufficient care to protect the best interests of a minor. When dealing with a minor, it is the psychologist's responsiblity to contact the parents directly. Written, informed consent of both parents and the child is advisable. The Committee voted to censure the psychologist and required that she take a course in scientific ethics at a local university.*

Case 5.d.2

Psychologist C was employed in a nursing home for the extremely elderly. He initiated a program to train the residents in self-management skills; to reinforce the lessons, he systematically withdrew privileges from those who failed to learn the skills taught. He anticipated that he would publish the results if they demonstrated that this model worked significantly better than those currently reported in the literature.

Another staff member criticized Psychologist C for his approach, arguing that some of those being deprived were too mentally frail to change their behavior under any circumstances. She submitted a complaint to the Ethics Committee after Psychologist C retorted to her criticism that, since the initiation of his program, self-management skills among the residents had significantly improved overall.

Psychologist C responded similarly to the Ethics Committee's inquiry, pointing to his program's success rate: According to his assessment, 23 of the 40 residents were now able to manage their lives more effectively than before the training. The administrator of the home confirmed that significantly fewer disruptions had occurred since the introduction of the program. Psychologist C asserted that the withholding of an hour of television privileges was an insignificant punishment compared to the self-management program's benefits. He explained that he had seen no reason to consult the institutional review board because the program did not involve research.

Adjudication: *The Ethics Committee found that Psychologist C had clearly violated Principle 5.d., entirely failing to take special care to protect the residents' best interests. The Committee censured him, determining that he should have used better screening techniques, obtained the institutional review board's approval of his program, and secured prior written consent from either the client involved or his or her legal representative.*

PRINCIPLE 6   **WELFARE OF THE CONSUMER**

General Principle: Psychologists respect the integrity and protect the welfare of the people and groups with whom they work. When conflicts of interest arise between clients and psychologists' employing institutions, psychologists clarify the nature and direction of their loyalties and responsibilities and keep all parties informed of their commitments. Psychologists fully inform consumers as to the purpose and nature of an evaluative, treatment, educational, or training procedure, and they freely acknowledge that clients, students, or participants in research have freedom of choice with regard to participation.

CASE 6.GP.1

Psychologist G was asked by the court to conduct a pre-sentencing psychological evaluation of Mr. H, which would be used to aid the court in deciding whether or not to sentence Mr. H to death. In Mr. H's state, the adjudication and sentencing phases of trials are separate, and he had already been convicted of the murder of two children.

Psychologist G met with Mr. H and informed him that the judge had asked her to perform an evaluation, which had as its purpose to obtain information that might affect whether or not he would get the death penalty. She further explained that in their state, the courts could consider certain psychological problems or histories as mitigating factors, lessening the likelihood of the death penalty, whereas other problems or histories could be considered aggravating factors, and so increase the likelihood of the death penalty. She explained that her role was to provide psychological data to the court, that the judge would make the ultimate decision, and that it was difficult to guess how a judge might interpret data. Furthermore, she said that she would not administer projective tests, because clients are not always aware of how much they reveal on such tests, and she wanted Mr. H to choose what to reveal in the evaluation. The district attorney, who had referred the case to Psychologist G, was so annoyed that she gave Mr. H such comprehensive information about the sentencing process and evaluation that he filed a complaint with the Ethics Committee.

Adjudication: *There was no dispute concerning the facts of the case. The Committee found that Psychologist G's behavior was not only ethical but exemplary in meeting Principle 6.b. and General Principle 6 as these relate to clarification of role and fully informed consent. These obligations are always important but are heightened when a psychologist's actions may have serious and even irreversible consequences for the client's life, as was the case in these legal proceedings. Whether the psychologist is performing an evaluation for a death penalty hearing, a custody hearing, or a competency hearing, basic civil and legal rights are at stake; the psychologist should fully inform the client as to the nature of the psychologist's role and the purposes of the evaluation.*

(Cross-reference to Principle 6.b., which obligates a psychologist who agrees to provide services to a client at the behest of a third party, to clarify the relationships involved to all parties.)

CASE 6.GP.2

Psychologist Q was asked by the court to conduct divorce mediation with a couple, Mr. and Mrs. P, concerning the custody of their child. Psychologist Q explained the goals and methods of mediation to the couple, stating that they would meet for eight sessions in an effort to reach a mutually satisfying custody arrangement. Conflict between the couple increased during the mediation. They failed to reach an agreement; thus, the matter was returned to the court for adjudication. Psychologist Q then voluntarily submitted a psychological evaluation report to the court, recommending that custody of the child be given to Mr. P. She reached this recommendation in part because he had been more conciliatory during the mediation attempt and therefore might be more likely than would Mrs. P to allow the children to have unobstructed visitation rights.

Mrs. P filed a complaint with the Ethics Committee concerning the report. Psychologist Q responded to the Committee's inquiry that she always submitted evaluation reports to the court after unsuccessful mediation and saw nothing wrong with doing so.

Adjudication: *The Committee found Psychologist Q in violation of General Principle 6 and Principle 6.a., for neither clarifying her role in the process nor fully informing the couple of the purpose and nature of their sessions. She failed to explain to Mr. and Mrs. P at the outset that she was serving in the dual role of mediator and evaluator. Nor did she inform Mr. and Mrs. P that the evaluative data provided by the mediation could be used in the custody adjudication, should one be necessary, as well as to help the couple reach an agreement. In addition, because Psychologist Q had released information from the sessions without either a court order or Mr. and Mrs. P's permission, she had also violated General Principle 5 relating to confidentiality.*
   The Ethics Committee censured Psychologist Q, and placed her forensic practice under the supervision of a boarded forensic psychologist, chosen by the Committee.

> (Cross-reference to General Principle 5, which obligates psychologists to respect the confidentiality of information obtained in the course of their work as psychologists; to Principle 6.a., which cautions psychologists to avoid exploiting their clients' trust; and to Principle 6.b., which requires psychologists who agree to provide services to a client at the request of a third party to clarify the relationships involved to all parties concerned.)

Principle 6.a.

Psychologists are continually cognizant of their own needs and of their potentially influential position vis-à-vis persons such as clients, students, and subordinates. They avoid exploiting the trust and dependency of such persons. Psychologists make every effort to avoid dual relationships that could impair their professional judgment or increase the risk of exploitation. Examples of such dual relationships include, but are not limited to, research with and treatment of employees, students, supervisees, close friends, or relatives. Sexual intimacies with clients are unethical.

Case 6.a.1

Ms. Y, a former client of Psychologist M, charged him with having engaged in a sexual relationship with her over the course of 18 months, during which period he continued to see her in a client relationship, treating her for depression within the context of marital problems. She accused Psychologist M of seducing her and luring her into an ongoing relationship by waiving fees for treatment and promising to testify for her in child custody hearings. Ms. Y stated that the relationship had been the final blow to her marriage and had cost her custody of her children to her former husband. Furthermore, the relationship had so traumatized her emotionally that she was now again in treatment, attempting to recover.

In response to the Ethics Committee's inquiry, Psychologist M confessed that he was guilty of having a sustained sexual relationship with Ms. Y while she was also his client. However, he claimed that Ms. Y had initiated the sexual contact, and that he had succumbed only after repeated propositions. Within a week of their first sexual encounter he found himself the object of blackmail. Ms. Y threatened him with public exposure, the destruction of his marriage and career, and on one occasion even swore to kill him. Psychologist M begged the Committee to understand that he had lived in constant terror of Ms. Y for a year and a half, continuing their sexual relationship only because the alternative appeared to be the destruction of his life.

After 18 months the guilt and fear proved physically overwhelming and he developed a bleeding ulcer. From his hospital bed he telephoned a prominent local clinician and asked his help. Psychologist M explained that he was now in treatment with Psychologist R, working on countertransference and other issues, and that he had placed his practice under Psychologist R's supervision.

Psychologist M admitted his guilt but begged committee members to consider the nightmare he had suffered, the efforts he was making to put his life back together, and the previous 25 years of a spotless career.

Adjudication: *The Ethics Committee found Psychologist M to have committed a serious violation of Principle 6.a. As he* *himself indicated, psychologists are expected to adhere to the highest standards with regard to sexual ethics. The Committee observed that neither the tragic personal consequences of his breach of the ethics code nor the depth of his remorse could absolve him of responsibility for his transgression and for accepting the consequences. The Committee recommended to the Board of Directors that Psychologist M be dropped from membership in APA. He appealed the recommendation, but it was upheld by a Board of Directors hearing panel, and the Board concurred with its finding.*

Case 6.a.2

Psychologist A was an adjunct university faculty member whose responsibilities included supervision of psychology graduate students' clinical work. Several times in the course of her supervision of Ms. B, they discussed how Ms. B's relationship with her father made it difficult for her to work with older male clients, focusing specifically on Ms. B's therapeutic effectiveness and case strategy. Psychologist A subsequently suggested to Ms. B that she consider entering psychotherapy to deal with her relationship with her father and other problems. Ms. B agreed, and thinking that Psychologist A's therapy model would be appropriate, she asked her supervisor to take her into her private practice. Psychologist A agreed to provide psychotherapy while continuing to supervise Ms. B and offered her a reduced fee, the only way the graduate student could afford psychotherapy. They set up regular sessions at Psychologist A's private office.

Following the receipt of a low grade for her clinical practicum with Psychologist A, the graduate student initiated ethics charges against her.

Adjudication: *The Ethics Committee censured Psychologist A for a violation of Principle 6.a. and ordered her to cease and desist any involvement in dual relationships. By entering into a formal psychotherapeutic relationship with Ms. B, Psychologist A created an unethical dual relationship. Dual relationships may impair professional judgment within both the roles (in this case, the roles of supervisor and therapist).*

Although the Committee understands that occasionally talking about a supervisee's personal problems as they affect therapeutic effectiveness in specific cases is permissible and often is an important aspect of clinical supervision, these discussions must remain restricted to the supervisor/super visee relationship. Many clinical programs include psycho therapy as an integral part of the training. It is imperative to select a therapist not otherwise involved with the student's graduate program.

Case 6.a.3

Psychologist C ran a psychotherapy group as a group process course offered to clinical psychology graduate students. As a member of the core clinical faculty, he taught other courses, provided research and clinical supervision to students, and served as a member of dissertation committees. He partici- pated in faculty discussions of students, evaluated their prog- ress, and helped make decisions about financial aid awards to students. A member of the group process course brought charges against Psychologist C, alleging that personal material the student had discussed in the course was used in his annual progress evaluation.

In response to the Ethics Committee's inquiry, Psychologist C denied that material from the group process course had been used in the student's progress evaluation. He admitted to serv- ing in multiple roles within the graduate program but explained that the faculty were relatively few in number.

Adjudication: *The Ethics Committee found Psychologist C in violation of Principle 6.a. Such situations, once common among graduate programs that required a psychotherapy experience, have serious potential for impaired professional judgment. Even had Psychologist C functioned in only one role in addition to that of therapist, the risk would have been high. Psychologist C was censured and sent a strongly worded educative letter from the Committee elaborating on the unac- ceptability of such dual relationships.*

Case 6.a.4

Psychologist D worked at a community mental health center as a clinician, in which capacity he did intake as well as psy- chotherapy. He saw Ms. E in an intake session and found her grieving her father's recent death. He recommended that she enter therapy with Psychologist F, a specialist in bereavement, and he arranged an appointment. In the intervening period, Psychologist D called Ms. E at home and inquired how she was getting along. Ms. E indicated that she was managing all right and agreed when Psychologist D asked if she would like to talk with him in his office that afternoon. At the end of the meeting, Psychologist D asked her on a date. They dated twice without sexual intimacies. Psychologist F later learned of the relationship and, with the permission of the client, filed a complaint with the Ethics Committee, alleging that Psychologist D had entered into a dual relationship with a client in violation of the *Ethical Principles*.

Psychologist D denied the charge, stating that he was not in a professional relationship with Ms. E at the time he asked her for a date. He stated that the referral to Psychologist F formally terminated their professional relationship. He contended that his invitation to his office for a second visit was not made in his professional role but in a new role as "friend or confidant." During that session they talked casually about himself and his own problems as well as her situation. He felt certain she understood that this was not a professional session.

Adjudication: *Although Psychologist D may have intended to enter into a purely personal relationship with Ms. E, it is likely that a client would not comprehend or be capable of making such an abrupt transition in roles. Although Psychologist D said that he had transferred to Psychologist F his formal professional responsibilities to Ms. E, it is not clear that this was the case since, at the time of the first telephone call, she had not yet seen Psychologist F.*

The Ethics Committee censured Psychologist D and mandated that he enter into treatment with a therapist of the Committee's choosing, the therapist to submit quarterly reports to the Committee. The treatment would focus on countertransference issues.

Case 6.a.5

Mr. S had once participated in business-related workshops with Psychologist X, after which they met for drinks a few times. Two years later Psychologist X called Mr. S to say that he had recently opened a private psychotherapy practice and was taking referrals. Mr. S confided that he and his wife were experiencing marital difficulties. Psychologist X indicated his willingness to see them. Mr. S was unsure whether his wife would agree, considering their earlier socializing. Psychologist X said he saw no problem because it had been more than 2 years and suggested that it might be easier to talk with an acquaintance than a stranger. Mr. S agreed and an appointment was arranged.

In the first session, Mrs. S stated that she doubted Psychologist X's ability to be fair and unbiased, given his previous friendship with her husband. Both Psychologist X and Mr. S assured her that no such relationship currently existed. Therapy proceeded, and Mrs. S repeatedly challenged Psychologist X's impartiality, stating that she felt his interpretations were biased toward her husband. These discussions began to consume most of the sessions. Finally, after talking with a member of the state psychological association staff, she terminated therapy and filed a complaint with the Ethics Committee.

Psychologist X denied any bias, contending that he did not have a dual relationship with the couple because they had not socialized during the past 2 years. He insisted that the *Ethical Principles* precluded professional relationships only with close friends. Finally, he stated that Mrs. S's obstructionist attitude was not a legitimate reaction to his passing friendship with her husband but a symptom of the problem she had with men that was causing their marital difficulties.

Adjudication: *The Ethics Committee concluded that Psychologist X had engaged in a dual relationship in violation of Principle 6.a., and in violation of Principle 6.e., had failed to terminate therapy and make an appropriate referral when it was clear that such action was in the client's best interest. The Committee concluded that because the conversation with Mr. S initiated by Psychologist X took place in a social context, Psychologist X could not claim that the social relationship had ended 2 years previously. Secondly, Psychologist X failed to heed Mrs. S's clear signals that she was not benefiting from the therapy relationship. This case emphasizes the important point that whether or not a therapist is actually biased, what matters is that the client perceives it to be so. Psychologist X was censured by the Committee.*

(Cross-reference to Principle 6.e., which obligates psychologists to terminate a clinical or consulting relationship when it is

reasonably clear the consumer is not
benefiting and to make an appropriate referral.)

Principle 6.b.

When a psychologist agrees to provide services to a client at
the request of a third party, the psychologist assumes the
responsibility of clarifying the nature of the relationships to
all parties concerned.

Case 6.b.1

The executive director of a mid-sized firm referred a very inef-
fectual employee of the firm to Psychologist Q for an evaluation. The administrator and the psychologist agreed prior to
the employee's first consultation that the psychologist would
report back to the administrator as to whether the psychological evaluation indicated that it was feasible for the employee
to continue in his position, and if so, whether remedial training
would improve his performance. The employee saw Psychologist Q for several sessions of interviews and testing, assuming
all that transpired during these sessions would be held confidential. Never doubting this, the employee did not raise questions about confidentiality and Psychologist Q did not explain
his arrangement with the firm.

Upon receipt of the psychologist's report, the executive
director preemptorily fired the employee. Realizing for the first
time what had occurred, the employee filed charges against
Psychologist Q with the Ethics Committee. Psychologist Q
responded to the Committee's inquiry that it was his understanding that the employer would brief the employee as to the
nature of the evaluation and its possible implications for his
continued employment with the firm. Assuming the company
would do so, Psychologist Q said he saw no reason to raise the
issue.

Adjudication: *The Ethics Committee found Psychologist Q
in violation of Principle 6.b., having obviously failed to fulfill
his responsibility to clarify to the client the nature of the
relationships between the three parties. Regardless of what
the psychologist understood to be the employer's plans, it
remained his ethical responsibility to be clear and explicit
himself with the client. The Committee censured him.*

Case 6.b.2

The adult daughter of a well-to-do couple entered treatment with Psychologist C presenting symptoms of severe depression. The parents paid for their daughter's treatment. All parties—the daughter, the psychologist, and the parents—agreed prior to the first session that the relationship between the therapist and her client would be held in confidence and that information regarding psychotherapy would not be revealed to the parents without the client's written consent.

Six months after the beginning of treatment the parents became concerned that their daughter's behavior had become more erratic. The client's mother began to press Psychologist C to divulge details of the sessions, insisting that she was frightened and desperate for information that would help her to cope and to understand how to support her daughter. The client absolutely refused to agree to her mother's having any information about her treatment. Psychologist C repeatedly refused the mother's demands for information, and eventually the mother filed a complaint with the Ethics Committee.

In response to the Committee's inquiry, Psychologist C explained that the agreement between the parties was absolutely clear from the beginning; that the confidentiality of the treatment could not be abridged without either the client's permission or the presence of substantial danger to the client or some other party. Although the mother alleged that she feared her daughter was becoming suicidal, the psychologist stated that it was her clinical opinion that no such danger existed.

Adjudication: *The Ethics Committee found that Psychologist C had acted so as to uphold Principle 6.b. of the* Ethical Principles, *clarifying relationships at the outset of treatment and adhering to that agreement. The Committee also agreed with Psychologist C's finding of no substantial danger and agreed to dismiss the charges. Even if there had been a real danger of suicide, the decision as to whether to inform a parent would still have been discretionary, and so failure to inform the parent would not necessarily have been unethical.*

Principle 6.c.

Where the demands of an organization require psychologists to violate these *Ethical Principles*, psychologists clarify the nature of the conflict between the demands and these principles. They inform all parties of psychologists' ethical responsibilities and take appropriate action.

Case 6.c.1

Psychologist J was hired as a researcher by a clinical agency. Initially, her function was to design an evaluative study that would compare the efficacy of two therapeutic modalities for treating depression: a behavioral group program and a psychotropic medication program with supportive psychotherapy. The clinic usually made client assignments to treatment based on the availability of therapists rather than any assessment of the preferred treatment for a particular client.

During the evaluation study the clinic wanted to assign clients randomly to one treatment or the other. Psychologist J pointed out that informed consent is required for randomization and for participation in the study's intervention and evaluation process. The clinic director, not an APA member, replied that the clinic did not have to inform clients they were participating in a research project because the random assignment process would be operationally similar to the former assignment system. The research psychologist was concerned about this decision but was hesitant to jeopardize her position. Psychologist J asked the Ethics Committee for guidance in this matter.

Opinion: The Committee responded to Psychologist J that she had a responsibility to comply with the *Ethical Principles* and any applicable state or federal regulations. For Psychologist J to continue her involvement with this project, she would have to convince the clinic to agree to the informed consent requirements or force compliance by filing a complaint with APA or the appropriate state body.

Case 6.c.2

The state education agency employed Psychologist W to do psychotherapy with its employees. The director of that agency received a request from another agency for details of a certain employee's treatment by Psychologist W. The representative of the second state agency, the bureau that handled foster child placements, explained that the employee had filed a request for services with the bureau and that it was believed the details of his treatment would help determine the favorable disposition of his request. The director of the state education agency forwarded the request for information from the foster children's bureau to Psychologist W. He refused to comply, after consulting with the employee in question, who did not wish to give his permission for the release of any information about his treatment to the foster children's bureau. When Psychologist W refused a second request, the director suspended him from his job and brought a complaint against him with the Ethics Committee. The complaint alleged a violation of General Principle 6, in that Psychologist W had failed to act in his client's best welfare.

Psychologist W responded to the Committee's inquiry that he had explained to the director his ethical responsibility as a psychologist to maintain the confidentiality of his client's treatment unless the client agreed to disclosure, which in this instance the client had clearly refused to do. There might be confusion as to which action would be in the client's best interests, but the client had understood his right to waive confidentiality had he wished to do so.

Adjudication: *The Committee dismissed the charges against Psychologist W, finding no violation of General Principle 6 and instead a careful adherence to Principle 6.c.*

Principle 6.d.

Psychologists make advance financial arrangements that safeguard the best interests of and are clearly understood by their clients. They neither give nor receive any remuneration for referring clients for professional services. They contribute a portion of their services to work for which they receive little or no financial return.

Case 6.d.1

Ms. Y was referred to Psychologist X, who had a private psychotherapy practice in which he charged $120 a session. Ms. Y expressed concern over her ability to pay and requested a referral to a therapist with a sliding scale. Psychologist X told her not to worry about the fee and to pay what she could. After several therapy sessions, Ms. Y brought up the fee issue again, reporting preoccupation with her mounting bill. Psychologist

X again told her not to worry but eventually the fee became the central topic of discussion in the sessions. Ms. Y suggested that since she had secretarial skills, she perhaps could work off the fee by typing manuscripts that Psychologist X was preparing for his new book. Psychologist X agreed. At first Ms. Y worked 20 hours per week, but the debt grew faster than she could earn money. Psychologist X then asked her to work 40 hours per week and to terminate therapy until she had paid the $3,000 bill, a period of nearly 4 months during which she was not in any treatment. She was not a skilled typist and he asked her to redo many sections. Having paid off the debt, on the advice of a friend who was a psychiatric nurse, she filed an ethics charge against Psychologist X.

Psychologist X denied any unethical behavior, stating that the typing arrangement was intended to benefit rather than to exploit Ms. Y. He argued that it was better for her to remain in therapy than to terminate, and that he believed a referral would have been premature. He stated that he had disapproved of her terminating therapy while she was working off the debt, but that she had become so agitated about the money that he had complied with her request. He had not foreseen that financial issues would interfere with therapy to the extent that they did.

Adjudication: *The Ethics Committee found that Psychologist X had violated several principles of the ethics code. He should have reduced his fee (Principle 6.d.) or made an appropriate referral to another therapist who could better meet the client's treatment needs (Principle 6.e.); instead he presented her with a vague arrangement that encouraged both parties to ignore financial realities. Had he reduced his fee, she would have had a clear and affordable goal for payment. Even if Psychologist X had not foreseen that the mounting debt would interfere with therapy, he should have heeded the many distress signals his client sent out as financial issues consumed more of each therapy session. There was additional evidence that he failed to evaluate carefully his client's need for continuing treatment when she asked to terminate therapy because of the financial pressure (Principle 6.e.). As General Principle 1 states, psychologists are expected to foresee and take responsibility for the consequences of their acts. Finally, bartering services (performing secretarial work in return for receiving therapy) violates Principle 6.a. by involving the psychologist in a dual relationship as both therapist and employer to the* *client. The Committee censured Psychologist X and placed him on a 3-year probation.*

(Cross-reference to Principle 6.a., which
forbids psychologists to engage in dual
relationships, and to Principle 6.e., which
requires psychologists to make a referral if a
client is clearly not benefiting from
treatment.)

Case 6.d.2

A psychologist initiated treatment with a client under a mutually agreed to rate of $70 per session. After several weeks of treatment, the client notified the psychologist by telephone the morning of their regular session that he was unexpectedly tied up in court and would be unable to make the session. The client was furious when he received his monthly statement from the psychologist to see that he had been charged for the missed session. He confronted the psychologist, who said that this was standard practice in the therapeutic community and that surely an educated person such as her client was aware of this practice.

The client submitted a complaint to the Ethics Committee, alleging that he had given the psychologist due notice that he would have to miss the session and that there had been no mutual agreement that the client would have to pay for cancelled sessions. The psychologist responded to the Ethics Committee's inquiry, as she had to the client, that this was standard practice in the community and that the client should certainly have expected it.

Adjudication: *The Ethics Committee found the psychologist in violation of Principle 6.d. for failing to ensure that all financial arrangements were clear to the client before treatment began. The Committee reprimanded the psychologist, demanded that she revoke the charge for the missed session, and charged that she be more explicit with her clients in the future.*

Principle 6.e.

Psychologists terminate a clinical or consulting relationship when it is reasonably clear that the consumer is not benefiting from it. They offer to help the consumer locate alternative sources of assistance.

Case 6.e.1

Psychologist G had been seeing a particular client for almost 9 years in "supportive therapy." Each time the client suggested termination, the psychologist strongly urged the client to continue in treatment, as "your ego defenses are simply not up to coping," predicting dire consequences if the client were to terminate.

The client began to feel the psychologist's treatment was unhelpful but was afraid to terminate the relationship or even discuss the matter with the psychologist. At the suggestion of a friend the client wrote to the Ethics Committee asking for help in determining whether or not he should terminate the relationship.

Adjudication: *When Psychologist G learned that the client had written to the Committee, he initiated the process of terminating therapy. The client was unwilling to file a complaint against the psychologist and therefore no official action could be taken. The Committee wrote an educative letter to the psychologist suggesting that, without questioning the psychologist's clinical judgment in this particular case, he should regularly review the issue of termination with clients, particularly with such long-term clients.*

Case 6.e.2

Psychologist D terminated a client's treatment because of a dispute over payment of the client's bill. The client requested the psychologist to identify another therapist and to send the client's records to the new therapist. Psychologist D refused both requests, demanding a full settlement of the bill before she would provide any future assistance. The client then wrote to the Ethics Committee.

Adjudication: *Although the client evidently had failed to meet his financial obligations to the therapist, the Committee concluded that the welfare of the client required that the psychologist help the client find a suitable new therapist and send his records—once a signed release was obtained—to that*

therapist. Holding records hostage to payment is not considered in the best interests of the client. Considering the dilemma,
however, no disciplinary action was taken against the psychologist once she agreed to follow the Committee's request
to send the records to the new therapist.

PRINCIPLE 7   **PROFESSIONAL RELATIONSHIPS**

General Principle: Psychologists act with due regard for the needs, special competencies, and obligations of their colleagues in psychology and other professions. They respect the prerogatives and obligations of the institutions or organizations with which these other colleagues are associated.

CASE 7.GP.1

Psychologist A agreed to write a chapter for a book edited by Psychologist B, for which the latter promised to pay $100. Psychologist A submitted a final revised chapter to Psychologist B in January of 1983. The book was eventually published in December of 1986 after delays caused by a change in publisher. After 5 months Psychologist A had received no payment, so he contacted the publisher who responded that the company had paid Psychologist B, who in turn should have compensated Psychologist A.

Psychologist A then contacted Psychologist B, who promised payment immediately. Another 6 months passed and no payment was received despite numerous phone calls and letters. Psychologist A wrote to Psychologist B notifying her that he was submitting a complaint to the Ethics Committee. In response to the Committee's letter notifying Psychologist B of the complaint, Psychologist B sent Psychologist A a letter of apology, payment for the chapter, and a small additional amount to cover the cost of telephone calls and interest.

Adjudication: *The Committee judged that Psychologist B had an obligation by prior agreement to pay Psychologist A for his professional work and had shirked her professional responsibility by not doing so promptly. A letter of reprimand was sent to Psychologist B stating that she had acted in violation of General Principle 7.*

(Cross-reference to Principle 7.g., which
suggests that psychologists attempt to resolve
relatively minor ethical violations informally.)

CASE 7.GP.2

Psychologist D and Psychologist E had for many years opposed each other's position on the theory that hypnosis can be used to reduce phobic responses. Their scientific disagreement had quickly turned into personal antipathy. In the midst of a social gathering that followed a symposium on the applications of hypnosis, Psychologist D loudly asserted that Psychologist E had been dropped from a graduate program for inadequate performance in the early 1970s and subsequently had been fired from a mental health clinic for sexually harassing a male clerical employee.

Psychologist E brought a complaint to the Ethics Committee about the incident, alleging a violation of General Principle 7. The Ethics Committee consulted with the psychologists who chaired the graduate program currently and at the time of the alleged dismissal. Both checked through the relevant documents and their personal records and reached the same conclusion: Psychologist E had voluntarily withdrawn from the program for personal financial reasons. Psychologist E confirmed that he had left the program to work for a few years in order to earn money and think over his career plans. He subsequently completed his graduate studies in another degree program.

The Committee also contacted the psychiatrist who directed the mental health clinic from which Psychologist E had allegedly been fired. The director found that Psychologist E had voluntarily left the clinic after 2 years, during which time his performance evaluations had been excellent.

Adjudication: *When the Ethics Committee contacted Psychologist D, she responded that the veracity of her sources was unimpeachable, but she refused to divulge their names because she felt obligated to protect them from reprisals. The Committee replied that because it could find no evidence to support Psychologist D's statements, it would be forced to take action if she would not provide the Committee with such evidence. She refused. The Committee censured Psychologist D for a violation of General Principle 7, because her appar-*

ently slanderous statements clearly reflected disrespect for Psychologist E's special competencies.

(Cross-reference to General Principle 3, which mandates psychologists to consider the impact of their public behavior on a colleague's ability to perform professional duties.)

Principle 7.a.

Psychologists understand the areas of competence of related professions. They make full use of all the professional, technical, and administrative resources that serve the best interests of consumers. The absence of formal relationships with other professional workers does not relieve psychologists of the responsibility of securing for their clients the best possible professional service, nor does it relieve them of the obligation to exercise foresight, diligence, and tact in obtaining the complementary or alternative assistance needed by clients.

Case 7.a.1

A psychologist in solo private practice was treating a moderately disturbed woman who was having problems at work with her supervisor. She was also having marital difficulties and was considering a divorce. Her husband did not want a divorce and independently started seeing another therapist who was a social worker. The social worker contacted the psychologist to request information and suggest either a conference with the psychologist alone or with the husband and wife as well. The psychologist refused to discuss the case with the social worker, saying that the patient had her own problems to be worked on that were independent of the marital situation. Furthermore, she said the practice and experience of the two therapists were so dissimilar that they probably could not work together on the case, and she discontinued the contact. The social worker initiated a complaint against the psychologist, who responded to the Committee reiterating what she had earlier told the social worker.

Adjudication: *The psychologist was advised by the Ethics Committee that her response to the social worker was inappropriate. She received a strong educative letter stating that,* *at the very least, she should have explored ways in which the two therapists could work together, and after obtaining her client's permission, have discussed relevant aspects of her situation with the social worker.*

Case 7.a.2

A middle-aged man suffering severe bouts of depression entered into treatment with a psychologist. After 18 months of psychotherapy, the client had seen no significant alleviation of his symptoms. Meanwhile he had read extensively in the popular literature about depression and experimental treatments for the illness. Convinced that his symptoms matched those of bipolar depression, the client asked for a referral for medication. The psychologist refused to make a referral, insisting that medication was not necessary, that the client was improving, and that his insistence on medication was simply a symptom of lingering resistance to the psychologist's authority.

The client abruptly stopped treatment with the psychologist and went to a social worker for therapy. She immediately referred him for medication. Over the course of several months the client's depression lifted, and he decided to bring charges against the psychologist with the Ethics Committee.

Adjudication: *The psychologist refused to respond to the Ethics Committee's inquiry. The Committee would have censured him for a violation of Principle 7.a., because it was convinced on the basis of available evidence that a referral for possible medication was warranted in this case, and that the psychologist had failed to secure services in the best interests of the client. However, because of the blatant refusal to cooperate, the Committee dropped the psychologist from membership in APA for noncooperation with the Ethics Committee, a violation of the Preamble to the* Ethical Principles.

(Cross-reference to the Preamble to the *Ethical Principles,* which sets forth the psychologist's obligation to cooperate with the APA Ethics Committee.)

Principle 7.b.

Psychologists know and take into account the traditions and practices of other professional groups with whom they work and cooperate fully with such groups. If a person is receiving similar services from another professional, psychologists do not offer their own services directly to such a person. If a psychologist is contacted by a person who is already receiving similar services from another professional, the psychologist carefully considers that professional relationship and proceeds with caution and sensitivity to the therapeutic issues as well as the client's welfare. The psychologist discusses these issues with the client so as to minimize the risk of confusion and conflict.

Case 7.b.1

A psychiatrist who was treating a 12-year-old boy complained to the Ethics Committee that the psychologist treating the boy's older sister had interfered in the younger boy's treatment. The psychiatrist stated that the psychologist had done a psychological evaluation of her client and had made recommendations about the boy's placement without consulting the psychiatrist.

The psychologist responded that his client was the legal guardian of her younger brother and had initiated the referral herself, without his prompting, because she was worried about her brother's worsening condition. His client had told him that after several attempts to talk with her younger brother, the boy had broken down, sobbing that he was scared of the psychiatrist. The older sister then asked whether he had told the psychiatrist he was scared, and the boy became more agitated, saying he was too afraid. He kept repeating that he was scared and was sure that if he told anyone the psychiatrist would hurt him. The boy showed such real distress that the older sister had sought her own therapist's assistance, asking him to perform an evaluation of her brother without notifying the psychiatrist. Although he obviously knew the boy was in treatment with another therapist, because of the circumstances the psychologist had acceded to his client's request, performing the evaluation and making the recommendation without notifying the psychiatrist.

Adjudication: *The Ethics Committee found that the psychologist had not committed a violation of Principle 7.b. His actions were based on evidence that indicated the possibility of jeopardy to the welfare of a minor. The psychologist had* *proceeded cautiously and carefully with sensitivity to the therapeutic and professional issues involved.*

Case 7.b.2

A psychologist was approached by a potential client, who had for more than a year participated in a therapy group led by a psychiatrist. The client proposed that he continue in the therapy group and also enter individual treatment with the psychologist. He did not plan to tell the psychiatrist that he had taken this step and insisted that the psychologist not inform the psychiatrist either. For 6 months the client continued in group therapy with the psychiatrist and individual therapy with the psychologist until one day the client inadvertently mentioned his individual work during a group session. The psychiatrist immediately brought an ethics charge against the psychologist.

In response to the Ethics Committee's inquiry, the psychologist responded that he felt no obligation to inform the psychiatrist that he had begun individual therapy with the client because it was obvious that both courses of treatment were proceeding well. Moreover, the client's reports made it clear that he was well satisfied with the progress of his treatments.

When contacted by the Ethics Committee, the client supported the psychologist's response in all respects. He added that he had chosen this course of action because he knew the psychiatrist had a firm policy that no one in the group could receive treatment outside the group; however, he was convinced that he needed individual treatment as well and now believed the subsequent course of his therapy supported his conviction.

Adjudication: *Because no damage had been done to the client, the Committee did not find a violation of Principle 7.b. However, the Committee did feel that the psychologist's behavior failed to meet the highest standards of professional conduct and strongly admonished him in the future to coordinate his work with other professionals carefully whenever possible conflicts should arise.*

Principle 7.c.

Psychologists who employ or supervise other professionals or professionals in training accept the obligation to facilitate the further professional development of these individuals. They provide appropriate working conditions, timely evaluations, constructive consultation, and experience opportunities.

Case 7.c.1

A recent Ph.D. in psychology complained of unfair treatment as a graduate student. She alleged that the examiners had given her an "invalid" question on her comprehensive examination, and that neither her advisor nor other faculty members appropriately encouraged her during graduate training. She repeated that examination and passed; however, she was not permitted to see the written evaluations by the three faculty members who graded the original examination she had failed.

Responding to the Ethics Committee about the complainant's allegations, her advisor indicated that it was departmental policy not to return comprehensive examinations to students. He pointed out, however, that he had discussed the evaluations with her at length in his office. He also cited from his own log and departmental records the number of contacts he had had with the student over the years.

Adjudication: *The Ethics Committee felt that it was beyond its charge to determine the validity of comprehensive examination questions—doubting whether there is any adequate measure of their validity—and found sufficient evidence that the department gave reasonable attention to this student and her problems. The Committee also noted that she had eventually passed her examinations and been awarded the degree. It found insufficient evidence to sustain a charge of violation of the* Ethical Principles.

Case 7.c.2

A clinical psychologist in postdoctoral supervision complained to the Ethics Committee that he had been preemptorily removed by his supervisor from a case. He had been working with a severely suicidal young woman and alleged that the interruption in treatment had seriously endangered her health.

In response to the Ethics Committee, the supervisor replied that she had removed the complainant from the case as alleged. He had not only refused to accept her supervision but had engaged in a number of seriously antitherapeutic behaviors.

On several occasions he had failed to show up for appointments with the client. He had ridiculed the client for the disarray of her marital affairs and directly accused her of using suicide threats to punish her husband for his infidelity. It was after one of the missed appointments that the client walked into the supervisor's office and asked for help. The supervisor immediately talked with the client and made a subsequent appointment with her, during which the supervisor explained that she was removing the postdoctoral psychologist from the case and offered the client an appointment the following day with one of the staff psychologists. The client readily agreed to the new arrangement.

Adjudication: *The Ethics Committee found that the supervisor had not committed a violation of Principle 7.c., but rather had acted in the client's best interests. Furthermore, by refusing to accept supervision, the complainant had made it impossible for the supervisor to consider his professional development in this case.*

Principle 7.d.

Psychologists do not exploit their professional relationships with clients, supervisees, students, employees, or research participants sexually or otherwise. Psychologists do not condone or engage in sexual harassment. Sexual harassment is defined as deliberate or repeated comments, gestures, or physical contacts of a sexual nature that are unwanted by the recipient.

Case 7.d.1

Three students accused a psychology professor, a popular lecturer on human sexuality and adult development, of making demeaning, sexist, and personal remarks during his lectures. When the students directly asked the professor to cease this behavior, pointing out that he was engaging in sexual harassment, he dismissed their request with a joke about female hormones and emotional overreaction.

The students submitted a formal complaint to the Ethics Committee after an incident in which the professor, during a lecture on coercion and sexual relationships, drew the attention of the class to an undergraduate female student who was wearing a halter top and shorts. He stated that dressed as she was, the student illustrated the phenomenon known as "jail bait."

When contacted by the Ethics Committee, the psychologist responded that he had made similar remarks during classes throughout his career. His comments about students were always humorous, meant to illustrate substantive points and to involve students personally. The professor added that he believed the complaint against him was a matter of feminist politics. He observed that the student about whom he had commented had not complained. He also noted that his ratings by students over the years were among the highest in the department.

Adjudication: *The Ethics Committee found that the professor's repeated and demeaning sexist comments clearly constituted sexual harassment of students and ordered him to cease and desist from making any such statements in the future. His failure to recognize the import of his remarks and his good intentions were irrelevant in this context. The professor accepted the Committee's letter of reprimand by stating that he would conform his conduct to its requirement.*

Case 7.d.2

A graduate student in psychology had received an appointment as a teaching assistant in the program. Her primary duties were to assist one of the major professors in teaching a large lecture course in educational psychology to undergraduates. Midway through the first semester of her assignment she received a telephone call at 3 a.m. from the professor. He complained that he had caught the flu from which she had been suffering the previous week, and that he was having painful back spasms. He invited her to come over and give him a back massage, joking that it was her responsibility to do so because she had given him the illness. She politely refused, not feeling comfortable in expressing her anger at receiving this request.

Distraught, the student contacted the Ethics Office for advice. She was afraid to bring charges until she had completed her doctoral program, for fear that the professor would retaliate and that he was sufficiently powerful within the department and the profession to ruin her career.

Opinion: The Ethics Office advised the student that because she was not a member of APA she had 5 years following an alleged ethics violation to bring a formal charge with the Ethics Committee. The student thanked the Ethics Office and said that she would bring charges immediately after she received her degree.

Principle 7.e.

In conducting research in institutions or organizations, psychologists secure appropriate authorization to conduct such research. They are aware of their obligation to future research workers and ensure that host institutions receive adequate information about the research and proper acknowledgment of their contributions.

Case 7.e.1

A clinical psychologist working as a counselor in a church affiliated family agency wanted to study the relationship between patterns of child care and attitudes toward contraception and abortion. Fearful that the agency might not approve her research, she inserted an attitude questionnaire into the standard intake procedure—which she supervised—without notifying the agency director or receiving official permission. She later justified her action on the basis of the study's importance. An intake employee at the agency reported the matter to the Ethics Committee.

Adjudication: *The Ethics Committee felt that the potential importance of the research could never outweigh the ethical requirement that the psychologist gain prior approval from the organization before embarking on a research project that used their clients. The Committee voted to reprimand the psychologist.*

Case 7.e.2

A school psychologist was personally interested in ways of improving intelligence. She conjectured that one way to do this would be to train children how to answer the questions on standard intelligence tests, such as the Wechsler Intelligence Scale for Children–Revised (WISC–R) intelligence test for children. She reasoned that the training would enable the

102

children to answer more questions correctly, improving their scores and making them feel better about themselves. Children with more self-esteem, she further reasoned, would actually be more intelligent human beings.

Eager to test her hypothesis, the psychologist obtained appropriate written releases from the parents or guardians of 25 children in the school where she was employed. She taught this sample of children the correct answers to the IQ test questions, and their scores subsequently were substantially higher. A colleague within the school system heard about the psychologist's actions and brought charges against her with the Ethics Committee, arguing that the psychologist had contaminated the IQ test for use with this population of children.

The school psychologist responded to the Ethics Committee's inquiry that she felt the goals of her study to have been admirable. She was working with a population of children with markedly low self-esteem. Recent emigrants from the poverty-stricken rural hill country surrounding the city, they were taunted by their classmates and severely handicapped by generations of educational deprivation. She insisted that it was essential to make these children feel better about themselves if they were to have any chance to succeed in the school system and later as adults in American society. She pointed out that there were other IQ tests that could be used in the event it were necessary to test these children.

Adjudication: *The Ethics Committee reprimanded the psychologist, arguing that although there were other IQ tests, the psychologist's actions precluded the application of the IQ test most commonly used with this population in future research, a violation of Principle 7.e. It also noted a possible breach of test security, a violation of the* Ethical Principles *under General Principle 8. The Committee noted that there were probably many other ways to improve self-esteem and that falsely inflating IQ scores may have been detrimental to the children in the long run.*

> (Cross-reference to General Principle 8, which requires psychologists to maintain the security of tests and other assessment techniques.)

Principle 7.f.

Publication credit is assigned to those who have contributed to a publication in proportion to their professional contributions. Major contributions of a professional character made by several persons to a common project are recognized by joint authorship, with the individual who made the principal contribution listed first. Minor contributions of a professional character and extensive clerical or similar nonprofessional assistance may be acknowledged in footnotes or in an introductory statement. Acknowledgment through specific citations is made for unpublished as well as published material that has directly influenced the research or writing. Psychologists who compile and edit material of others for publication publish the material in the name of the originating group, if appropriate, with their own name appearing as chairperson or editor. All contributors are to be acknowledged and named.

Case 7.f.1

A professor who had obtained a large grant employed a graduate student as a research assistant, whom he paid the prevailing rate for graduate assistants in the department. The student's duties included running subjects, tabulating data, doing statistical analyses with packaged programs, and completing a literature review. The professor wrote a series of articles based on the results of the study and gave the student footnote credit. The student complained to the Ethics Committee that he should have been listed as an author.

The professor responded that the student had been adequately paid for his services and had in no way been involved with the basic theory or design of the experiment or with obtaining the grant. He was only minimally involved in preparing the manuscript, having proofread and looked up references.

Adjudication: *The Ethics Committee found insufficient evidence to sustain a charge of violation of the* Ethical Principles. *Whether or not the student had been paid for his work was irrelevant. To warrant credit as an author, a psychologist has to contribute significantly to the design, analyses, and writing of a report. The evidence indicated that the student had made only a minor contribution to the substantive aspects of the research and therefore was adequately acknowledged in a footnote.*

Three colleagues worked together over the course of several years on a study of communicative behavior between mammals belonging to a particular subspecies native to arctic climates. They prepared an article for submission to a leading psychological journal and ranked themselves in authorship in the order agreed to at the outset of the study, which they had anticipated would reflect their relative contributions. The first author embarked on a 6-month tour of the Antarctic to pursue related research prior to the publication of the article. When the journal returned the manuscript to the first author's office for a final proofread, her secretary forwarded the manuscript to the second author. He reviewed the article and removed the third author, crediting his work instead in a footnote.

When the issue of the journal arrived in which their article was to have appeared, the third author was shocked to discover that he was no longer listed as an author. He was under consideration at the time for promotion by his university to full professor and had already added the article to his vita as a publication credit. Immediately upon the first author's return to the country, the third author questioned her about the article, and she was equally astounded. Together they submitted an ethics complaint against the second author to the Ethics Committee.

The second author responded to the Committee's inquiry that, despite their agreement at the outset of the project, the third author's contribution did not turn out to warrant authorship. He had performed as a technician, the second author alleged, simply following the directions given by the first and second authors. Although his technical assistance was useful to the project and so deserved a footnote, his role was not so significant that he had earned the authorship initially agreed to.

Adjudication: *The Ethics Committee found the second author's response entirely unconvincing. They determined that he had no right unilaterally to abridge the previous agreement pertaining to authorship. The Committee censured the second author for a violation of Principle 7.f. and required that he arrange for the journal that printed the article to publish an erratum.*

Principle 7.g.

When psychologists know of an ethical violation by another psychologist, and it seems appropriate, they informally attempt to resolve the issue by bringing the behavior to the attention of the psychologist. If the misconduct is of a minor nature and/or appears to be due to lack of sensitivity, knowledge, or experience, such an informal solution is usually appropriate. Such informal corrective efforts are made with sensitivity to any rights to confidentiality involved. If the violation does not seem amenable to an informal solution, or is of a more serious nature, psychologists bring it to the attention of the appropriate local, state, and/or national committee on professional ethics and conduct.

Case 7.g.1

A psychologist starting a private practice placed an advertisement in the classified telephone directory that listed her name, degree, certification by hypnotherapy and marital counseling institutes, and membership in APA, followed by a listing of specialties in boldface type: "Phobias, Fears, Insecurities, Sexual and Marital Problems." In smaller print was the notice "Diagnostic and therapeutic mental health services for children and adults."

The psychologist was informed by a colleague with whom she shared an office that the listing was in violation of Principle 4.b., in that she was advertising her APA membership in the context of her professional credentials, and as such the listing would be false and misleading. The psychologist wrote to the Ethics Office for an opinion.

Opinion: The Director of the Ethics Office, in consultation with several Ethics Committee members, determined that, because of its placement in the ad, the listing was indeed inappropriate. The psychologist replied that she had committed the infraction unwittingly and would immediately withdraw the listing from the directory. The case was closed without further adjudication.

Case 7.g.2

Psychologist G was reviewing the literature on sports psychology in preparation for a monograph she planned to write on the psychological stress experienced by college athletes of exceptional promise. In the process she discovered that major parts of two articles published by a colleague, Psychologist H, were plagiarized word-for-word from doctoral dissertations written by two of Psychologist G's students. Psychologist G immediately filed a complaint with the Ethics Committee, charging violations of Principles 1.a. and 7.f.

Informed of the charge by the Ethics Committee, Psychologist H attempted to file a countercharge under Principle 7.g., on the grounds that Psychologist G was obligated under that principle to deal with him personally about the charge and attempt to resolve the problem before taking it to APA. He further argued that until Psychologist G did so the entire matter was not properly in the domain of the Ethics Committee.

Adjudication: *The Ethics Committee responded, first, that it could not under its rules accept a countercomplaint under any circumstances while the initial complaint was under investigation. Secondly, under Principle 7.g., a psychologist who honestly and in good faith believes that a serious violation of the* Ethical Principles *has occurred is under no obligation to speak with the accused but may bring the matter directly to the Ethics Committee's attention. The Committee voted formal charges against Psychologist H for a violation of Principle 1.a., and the Board of Directors dropped him from membership.*

(Cross-reference to Principle 1.a., which mandates that psychologists take credit only for work they have actually done.)

PRINCIPLE 8 **ASSESSMENT TECHNIQUES**

General Principle: In the development, publication, and utilization of psychological assessment techniques, psychologists make every effort to promote the welfare and best interests of the client. They guard against the misuse of assessment results. They respect the client's right to know the results, the interpretations made, and the bases for their conclusions and recommendations. Psychologists make every effort to maintain the security of tests and other assessment techniques within limits of legal mandates. They strive to ensure the appropriate use of assessment techniques by others.

CASE 8.GP.1

A television program showed a psychologist administering the Rorschach test to a disturbed adolescent. The situation was portrayed as a spontaneous administration of the test: Each card was shown for about 5 seconds on the screen and then superimposed on the subject's face as she responded. The psychologist was identified by his real name; the subject was played by a professional actress and given a fictitious name. Another psychologist who saw the show brought charges.

When asked to reply to the complaint received by the Ethics Committee about the broadcast, the psychologist responded that the series of programs, presented by a major network, used mental health professionals as consultants and had been praised as a public service in a recent professional publication. The program was a fictionalized drama and used actors in all roles but the professionals. The psychologist had been asked to appear in a scene that depicted the administration of a psychological test, simply acting as though he were administering the test while the subject, a professional actress, acted as though she were responding. He had first discussed the invitation with colleagues and found that all respected the producer's integrity and regarded the program as an admirable attempt to acquaint the public with the ways in which mental health professions cooperate with the courts to serve society. He had been told that there would be brief close-up shots of the test situation and did not learn until after the telecast that the actual Rorschach cards had been shown. With his reply, he enclosed a copy of the letter he sent to the producer soon after the broadcast, informing her of the ethical considerations infringed upon and expressing chagrin at the way in which the simulated test had been handled.

Adjudication: *Because the value of psychological tests and other assessment devices depends in part on the naivete of the subject, the broadcast of Rorschach cards potentially compromised the validity of the technique for a significant sector of the population. Because it is the psychologist's responsibility "to make every effort to maintain the security of tests and other assessment techniques," the psychologist was held responsible for the inappropriate telecast of the Rorschach cards and found to have violated General Principle 8. However, the Committee closed the case without further action, in view of his good faith in entering the situation, his foresight in discussing the situation with colleagues before accepting the invitation, and his having fulfilled his responsibility to notify the network of the ethical significance of its action.*

CASE 8.GP.2

A toy manufacturing company particularly interested in painting and drawing materials invited a psychologist to develop a drawing test that could give parents "valuable information regarding the personality development of the child." The psychologist had been impressed by the amount of information obtained through children's drawings, particularly when supplemented by a questionnaire that she had used in private practice for many years. Before signing a contract with the firm, however, she wished to be certain that such an arrangement with a commercial enterprise was proper and queried the Ethics Committee as to whether the test could be given to parents.

Opinion: The Committee had no objection to the construction of the test but strongly objected to the plan for promoting the test to parents. It would be a violation of General Principle 8 to place such tests in the hands of anyone unskilled in their use and interpretation. The Committee indicated to the psychologist that her agreement with the company would have to specify that the material would be marketed and released only to trained and responsible professionals.

CASE 8.GP.3

A psychologist gave information about a figure-drawing test to a freelance writer, who was writing an article. The psychologist was under the impression that the article would be a dignified, general statement about how such tests help psychologists provide services to the public. Instead the article appeared in the magazine under the banner heading "Figure Out Your Own Personality." It provided blank space for drawings, gave instructions about scoring, and showed illustrative drawings. Many psychologists sent the article to the APA Ethics Office, complaining that the *Ethical Principles* had been violated.

Adjudication: *The Ethics Committee found the psychologist in technical violation of General Principle 8. Although the psychologist evidently did not intend to violate any ethical principle, he exercised poor judgment in underestimating the dangers inherent in popularizing projective techniques. For a popular magazine to publish projective or other tests with examples and interpretive guidelines invites self-application by inexperienced readers and may also invalidate the material for future use. A psychologist is responsible for careful judgment in making test materials available, for it is impossible to control their subsequent use. The psychologist received an educative letter to this effect from the Committee and the case was closed. He was further instructed to obtain a written statement describing goals, application, and intent of an author who plans to write an article based on an interview. He was also informed of the necessity of previewing the final work before it goes to press.*

Principle 8.a.

In using assessment techniques, psychologists respect the right of clients to have full explanations of the nature and purpose of the techniques in language the clients can understand, unless an explicit exception to this right has been agreed upon in advance. When the explanations are to be provided by others, psychologists establish procedures for ensuring the adequacy of these explanations.

Case 8.a.

A student completed a battery of tests at a university placement office. The report he received named all the tests that he had completed and gave percentile scores for each. No written or oral interpretation of the test results was provided. Distressed by the test results, the student sought help at the counseling center, where a psychologist who talked with the student discovered the source of the problem: In the absence of professional interpretation, the student had misconstrued the meaning of the scores. The psychologist suggested that the incident be reported to the Ethics Committee as a possible violation of the *Ethical Principles.*

Adjudication: *The Committee lacked jurisdiction in the matter because the person responsible for the error was not an APA member. The Committee, however, wrote to the head of the placement center suggesting that the practice of giving clients uninterpreted test scores had subjected this student to unfortunate and unnecessary emotional distress. The Eth-*ical Principles *do not prohibit giving test scores in the form of percentiles to a client but place responsibility on the psychologist to ensure that the client is able to understand the results as reported. Care must be taken that measures of aptitude, interest, and personality are not confused and misinterpreted by the client. This is often difficult to accomplish regardless of the form in which results are communicated, so it is usually wise to keep technical details to a minimum.*

Principle 8.b.

Psychologists responsible for the development and standardization of psychological tests and other assessment techniques utilize established scientific procedures and observe the relevant APA standards.

Case 8.b.

An APA member submitted to the Ethics Committee promotional material circulated in connection with a battery of tests developed by two other APA members. The Ethics Committee secured copies of the tests and raised questions with the test developers concerning both the appropriateness of the promotional statements and the degree to which the tests themselves met technical requirements. The psychologists involved promised to take steps to correct the promotional material and indicated that a technical manual for the test was in preparation.

The tests were then submitted by the Ethics Committee to a former member of the APA Committee on Psychological Tests and Assessments for evaluation. The reviewer found the tests seriously deficient in meeting technical requirements. The psychologists were invited to meet with an ad hoc fact-finding committee whose members were chosen on the basis of their knowledge about test construction and development. They sought to evaluate the psychologists' background and experience in test development as well as the technical adequacy of the tests themselves. The ad hoc committee found shortcomings on both scores. The psychologists showed inadequate understanding of basic testing principles, and the tests contained errors both of omission and commission.

Adjudication: *The ad hoc committee found several violations of the* Ethical Principles. *Deceptive promotional statements violate General Principle 4 and 4.e. The substandard tests were a violation of Principle 8.b. Both psychologists were practicing outside their area of competence in violation of General Principle 2. In response to these findings, the psychologists expressed their desire to comply with APA's standards and regulations, their willingness to cease and desist from further marketing of the tests, and their intent to terminate their contract with the publisher to develop the test. The ad hoc committee recommended that the psychologists be admonished and that charges be pressed if they failed either to bring the tests and marketing procedures in line with APA policy or suspend marketing the instruments in question. The Ethics Committee accepted the recommendations of the ad hoc committee; after receiving the necessary documentation that the conditions were complied with fully, the case was closed without further action.*

(Cross-reference to General Principle 2, which forbids psychologists to practice outside their areas of competence, and to General Principle 4 and to Principle 4.e., which bar psychologists from making inappropriate or scientifically inaccurate statements in their promotional materials.)

Principle 8.c.

In reporting assessment results, psychologists indicate any reservations that exist regarding validity or reliability because of the circumstances of the assessment or the inappropriateness of the norms for the person tested. Psychologists strive to ensure that the results of assessments and their interpretations are not misused by others.

Case 8.c.1

A psychologist in a large metropolitan school district contacted the Ethics Office for an opinion about the suitability of a testing and placement program in the school system about which he was concerned. The district based its placement decisions for entering students on the Wechsler Intelligence Scale for Children–Revised (WISC–R). His concern was that the test was used to assess and place newly arrived immigrant Puerto Rican children, who lacked any fluency in the English language and for whom there were no appropriate norms. As a result, many children were labeled mentally retarded and placed in special education classes.

Opinion: The Ethics Committee sent a letter to the psychologist to the effect that this kind of test usage could be seen as a violation of Principle 8.c. because of the inappropriateness of the norms and the language difficulties. When apprised of this difficulty the school stopped using the WISC–R with non-English speaking children and accepted the psychologist's offer to help them devise an alternate and more appropriate placement program.

(Cross-reference to Principle 6.c., which requires psychologists to clarify to all parties involved any conflict between an organization's demands and the *Ethical*

Principles; and to Principle 2.d., which requires that psychologists recognize differences among people, such as those that may be associated with age, sex, socioeconomic, and ethnic backgrounds. When necessary, they obtain training, experience, or counsel to assure competent service or research relating to such persons.)

Case 8.c.2

A high school student confused about his career goals and educational interests sought help from Psychologist F. Psychologist F administered a battery of vocational interest and ability tests to the student to try to help him set some direction for his college education. Six months later, at the beginning of the summer before the student planned to enter college, he went into therapy with Psychologist G because of the severe anxiety he had begun to experience about the prospect of leaving home and beginning college in another state. Psychologist G requested and received from Psychologist F copies of the interest and ability tests he had administered to the student. Psychologist G then wrote a detailed personality evaluation of the client based on the test results. Psychologist F later asked Psychologist G how the client was doing and whether the test results had been helpful in the therapy process. Learning for the first time how the test results had been used, Psychologist F queried Psychologist G about her procedure and, not satisfied with the response, brought a complaint with the Ethics Committee.

In response to the Committee's inquiry, Psychologist G was unable to give a rationale for the procedures she used to evaluate the student's personality based on interest and ability test results. Nor was she able to point to any research that supported her interpretive approach. However, she assured the Committee that her manner of proceeding in this case was intuitively sound, based on her 5 years' experience as a counselor and her training in test administration, and reflected the obvious connection between the client's anxiety and his vocational plans.

Adjudication: *The Ethics Committee disagreed with Psychologist G's rationale for her actions and reprimanded her, ordering her to cease and desist such conduct.*

Principle 8.d.

Psychologists recognize that assessment results may become obsolete. They make every effort to avoid and prevent the misuse of obsolete measures.

Case 8.d.1

An individual was denied promotion to a managerial position, based on an assessment report prepared by a psychologist 10 years previously. The assessment consisted of five psychological tests and an interview.

Responding to the individual's complaint to the Ethics Committee, the psychologist stated that she had worked for the employer on a consultant basis and was asked to assess the suitability of each individual tested for a sales or managerial position. The psychologist had submitted a report to the employer recommending that the individual be employed in a sales but not a managerial position. The psychologist stated that she had no control over how the employer used the reports submitted 10 years previously; however, she agreed that the employee should be reassessed for a managerial position.

Adjudication: *Because the psychologist no longer worked with the employer and was not consulted on this matter, the Ethics Committee did not hold her responsible for the employer's violation of the* Ethical Principles. *The Committee did suggest that the psychologist advise her former client that obsolete reports should be destroyed and employees reassessed when appropriate. In the future, she should establish a formal agreement that would establish guidelines for the use and retention of her reports.*

(Cross-reference to General Principle 8 and Principle 8.c., which require psychologists to guard against the misuse of assessment results.)

Case 8.d.2

The complainant alleged that he had applied at the age of 18 for a police officer position in his local community. He was referred to a psychologist for assessment. Subsequently, without explanation, he was turned down as "unfit" for the position. He then joined the U.S. Army and served for 8 years in the military police. After his discharge the complainant again applied for a police officer position. He was referred to the same psychologist who scanned his previous file and asked him a few questions concerning his Army service and his current situation. Soon thereafter, and again without explanation, he was turned down as unfit for the position. The psychologist affirmed that he had recommended, based on test scores and an interview, that the individual not be employed as a police officer. He stated that he saw no need to retest the individual and added that his service in the military police confirmed the psychologist's earlier conviction that he would be unfit for service in a civilian police department. The psychologist declined to explain his basis for this conclusion and contended furthermore that feedback to the applicant was not his responsibility; his client, the police department, had the option to provide such feedback in accordance with its policies and practices.

Adjudication: *The Ethics Committee found the psychologist in violation of Principle 8.d. for failure to reassess the individual for the position and censured him. It also required that he discuss the feedback issue with the police department, recommending feedback procedures to be used with future applicants.*

> (Cross-reference to Principle 6.c., which requires psychologists to inform all parties of ethical conflicts posed by disagreements between an organization's demands and the *Ethical Principles*, and to Principle 8.a., which requires psychologists to give their clients a full explanation of the nature and purpose of assessment techniques used; and to Principle 8.f., which states that psychologists should not encourage or promote the use of psychological assessment techniques by inappropriately trained or otherwise unqualified persons through teaching, sponsorship, or supervision.)

Principle 8.e.

Psychologists offering scoring and interpretation services are able to produce appropriate evidence for the validity of the programs and procedures used in arriving at interpretations. The public offering of an automated interpretation service is considered a professional-to-professional consultation. Psychologists make every effort to avoid misuse of assessment reports.

Case 8.e.1

A psychologist employed by a private clinic for emotionally disturbed children developed a test to assess certain aspects of brain damage. The test was similar to several other well-established instruments designed to measure brain damage, although not so similar as to constitute an infringement of copyright. The psychologist did not perform any studies to substantiate his test's validity. He set up a computer program to score and interpret the instrument. In marketing the program, he attached a disclaimer to the package to the effect that "validation efforts are continuing."

Another psychologist purchased the test and noticed the disclaimer as she began to try out the test for the first time. She brought charges against the first psychologist for a violation of the *Ethical Principles.*

In response to the Ethics Committee's inquiry, the first psychologist explained that he had attached the disclaimer to the computer program precisely to avoid this problem. He wished to be sure his colleagues realized when purchasing the program that the test was still in an experimental stage and that further validation studies remained to be done. He did not wish to deceive anyone and regretted that the complainant had not noticed the disclaimer before she purchased the test.

Adjudication: *The Ethics Committee reprimanded the first psychologist for a violation of Principle 8.e. and ordered him to cease and desist. He had marketed and offered scoring and interpretation services before validating the procedures used, while at the same time implying in his disclaimer that some validation studies had been performed.*

Case 8.e.2

A psychologist was hired by the fire department of a large suburban county to set up a procedure for selecting new hires from among the many applicants for firefighter positions. As part of the selection process the psychologist established, she used a computerized MMPI program that had proved useful in selecting candidates for firefighter positions. A year later, as a result of severe budget cutbacks, the fire department found it necessary to dispense with the psychologist's services and asked her to allow the department to continue to use the MMPI program. The psychologist was also asked to release all previous assessment results to the department and to train a nonprofessional to administer and interpret the program. The psychologist wrote to the Ethics Committee to ask if it would be ethical for her to comply with the fire department's requests.

Opinion: The Committee responded that to release either the program or the earlier assessments to persons not trained to interpret them would violate Principle 8.e. of the *Ethical Principles*. The psychologist thanked the Committee for its response and notified the fire department that she would be unable to do as they had requested.

> (Cross-reference to General Principle 8, which cautions the psychologist to guard against the misuse of test results and maintain the security of tests, and to General Principle 5, which obligates psychologists to respect the confidentiality of information obtained in their work as psychologists.)

Principle 8.f.

Psychologists do not encourage or promote the use of psychological assessment techniques by inappropriately trained or otherwise unqualified persons through teaching, sponsorship, or supervision.

Case 8.f.1

A graduate psychology student reported to the Committee that she had observed undergraduate students administering and interpreting the Rorschach test to other students in the dormitory where she was a resident advisor. She indicated that she had learned from one student that their instructor for an undergraduate course in individual differences had given them the Rorschach cards. When approached by the Ethics Committee about the matter, the psychologist said that he saw nothing wrong with giving such an assignment to undergraduates.

Adjudication: *The Committee found the assignment to be in violation of General Principle 8 and 8.f. and issued a reprimand to the psychologist. The Committee required him to cease and desist from such activity, and he agreed to do so.*

Case 8.f.2

A small liberal arts college offered several substantial awards annually to incoming freshmen that covered all tuition and expenses for 4 years of undergraduate study. In recent years two students who won these awards later encountered emotional difficulties so severe that they were unable to complete their undergraduate programs. To avoid such situations in the future, the college decided to add emotional stability to its criteria for selection for these awards. Because its resources were limited, the college hired a psychologist to train two members of the college infirmary staff to administer and interpret a battery of personality tests.

The parent of an applicant turned down for an award was told by his son that he had taken personality tests. When he learned that the infirmary staff had administered the tests and subsequently discovered the nature of their training, he brought an ethics charge against the psychologist who had trained the two nurses. In response to the Ethics Committee's inquiry, the psychologist replied that she had had no idea that her actions could have been construed as unethical; she had tried to train the nurses as well as she could and had given them her office phone number and urged them to call if any difficulties arose.

Adjudication: *The Ethics Committee was unconvinced that either the training or the supervision provided by the psychologist was adequate, nor were the members persuaded that the nurses' training or experience adequately qualified them to administer and interpret psychological tests. The Ethics Committee censured the psychologist and ordered her to work with the college to discontinue its testing program. The Committee also mandated that she take a graduate-level ethics course at a local university.*

PRINCIPLE 9 **RESEARCH WITH HUMAN PARTICIPANTS[1]**

General Principle: The decision to undertake research rests upon a considered judgment by the individual psychologist about how best to contribute to psychological science and human welfare. Having made the decision to conduct research, the psychologist considers alternative directions in which research energies and resources might be invested. On the basis of this consideration, the psychologist carries out the investigation with respect and concern for the dignity and welfare of the people who participate and with cognizance of federal and state regulations and professional standards governing the conduct of research with human participants.

a. In planning a study, the investigator has the responsibility to make a careful evaluation of its ethical acceptability. To the extent that the weighing of scientific and human values suggests a compromise of any principle, the investigator incurs a correspondingly serious obligation to seek ethical advice and to observe stringent safeguards to protect the rights of human participants.

b. Considering whether a participant in a planned study will be a "subject at risk" or a "subject at minimal risk," according to recognized standards, is of primary ethical concern to the investigator.

c. The investigator always retains the responsibility for ensuring ethical practice in research. The investigator is also responsible for the ethical treatment of research participants by collaborators, assistants, students, and employees, all of whom, however, incur similar obligations.

d. Except in minimal-risk research, the investigator establishes a clear and fair agreement with research participants, prior to their participation, that clarifies the obligations and responsibilities of each. The investigator has the obligation to honor all promises and commitments included in that agree-

---

[1]There are no cases listed for Principles 9 and 10 as there is a separate casebook being developed within the Office of Scientific Affairs for these two principles.

ment. The investigator informs the participants of all aspects of the research that might reasonably be expected to influence willingness to participate and explains all other aspects of the research about which the participants inquire. Failure to make full disclosure prior to obtaining informed consent requires additional safeguards to protect the welfare and dignity of the research participants. Research with children or with partici- pants who have impairments that would limit understanding and/or communication requires special safeguarding proce- dures.

e.   Methodological requirements of a study may make the use of concealment or deception necessary. Before conducting such a study, the investigator has a special responsibility to (i) determine whether the use of such techniques is justified by the study's prospective scientific, educational, or applied value; (ii) determine whether alternative procedures are available that do not use concealment or deception; and (iii) ensure that the participants are provided with sufficient explanation as soon as possible.

f.   The investigator respects the individual's freedom to decline to participate in or to withdraw from the research at any time. The obligation to protect this freedom requires care- ful thought and consideration when the investigator is in a position of authority or influence over the participant. Such positions of authority include, but are not limited to, situa- tions in which research participation is required as part of employment or in which the participant is a student, client, or employee of the investigator.

g.   The investigator protects the participant from physical and mental discomfort, harm, and danger that may arise from research procedures. If risks of such consequences exist, the investigator informs the participant of that fact. Research pro- cedures likely to cause serious or lasting harm to a participant are not used unless the failure to use these procedures might expose the participant to risk of greater harm, or unless the research has great potential benefit and fully informed and voluntary consent is obtained from each participant. The par- ticipant should be informed of procedures for contacting the investigator within a reasonable time period following partic- ipation should stress, potential harm, or related questions or concerns arise.

h.   After the data are collected, the investigator provides the participant with information about the nature of the study and attempts to remove any misconceptions that may have arisen. Where scientific or humane values justify delaying or withholding this information, the investigator incurs a special responsibility to monitor the research and to ensure that there are no damaging consequences for the participant.

i.   Where research procedures result in undesirable consequences for the individual participant, the investigator has the responsibility to detect and remove or correct these consequences, including long-term effects.

j.   Information obtained about a research participant during the course of an investigation is confidential unless otherwise agreed upon in advance. When the possibility exists that others may obtain access to such information, this possibility, together with the plans for protecting confidentiality, is explained to the participant as part of the procedure for obtaining informed consent.

PRINCIPLE 10 **CARE AND USE OF ANIMALS**[1]

General Principle: An investigator of animal behavior strives to advance understanding of basic behavioral principles and/or to contribute to the improvement of human health and welfare. In seeking these ends, the investigator ensures the welfare of animals and treats them humanely. Laws and regulations notwithstanding, an animal's immediate protection depends upon the scientist's own conscience.

a.   The acquisition, care, use, and disposal of all animals are in compliance with current federal, state or provincial, and local laws and regulations.

b.   A psychologist trained in research methods and experienced in the care of laboratory animals closely supervises all procedures involving animals and is responsible for ensuring appropriate consideration of their comfort, health, and humane treatment.

c.   Psychologists ensure that all individuals using animals under their supervision have received explicit instruction in experimental methods and in the care, maintenance, and handling of the species being used. Responsibilities and activities of individuals participating in a research project are consistent with their respective competencies.

d.   Psychologists make every effort to minimize discomfort, illness, and pain of animals. A procedure subjecting animals to pain, stress, or privation is used only when an alternative procedure is unavailable and the goal is justified by its prospective scientific, educational, or applied value. Surgical procedures are performed under appropriate anesthesia; techniques to avoid infection and minimize pain are followed during and after surgery.

e.   When it is appropriate that the animal's life be terminated, it is done rapidly and painlessly.

---

[1]There are no cases listed for Principles 9 and 10 as there is a separate casebook being developed within the Office of Scientific Affairs for these two principles.

GLOSSARY OF ETHICS COMMITTEE TERMS

TERM	DEFINITION
Appeal	There are two kinds of appeals. First, an appeal of a Reprimand or Censure entails the complainee's submitting a reason therefor; the Committee can then withdraw its action, have an informal hearing, or submit the materials to three members of the Appeal Panel each of whom independently reviews the materials and votes to uphold the Committee, withdraw the sanction, or continue to investigate. A majority vote is binding. An appeal of a recommendation to drop someone from membership can go before three members of the Hearing Panel in a formal hearing (in the District of Columbia) who then make a recommendation to the Board of Directors, a recommendation which is typically binding.
Appeal Panel	The appeal panels are drawn from a list of approximately 25 persons, psychologists and nonpsychologists, who comprise the Board of Directors Standing Hearing Panel. These persons, none of whom can be current members of the Committee, are selected by the President and the Director for their expertise in ethics.
Bar Resignation	A routine procedure which prohibits a member's resignation from APA when either a case is opened, or the Office is notified that an APA member is being investigated by a state association. This maintains APA jurisdiction until there is a resolution to the matter.
Case Monitor	Each of the cases when it is opened is assigned to one member of the Committee to be the backstop for the office in the investigation of that particular case. A person so assigned is called the case monitor for that case.
Censure	A censure is implemented by the Committee when it feels that there has been an infraction of the ethics code, there has been some damage done to another person but that damage is not sufficient to warrant dropping the psychologist from membership in the APA.

Check List

The Ethics Complaint Check List is the basic complaint form which has to be filled out before we take any action on a case. It includes the who, when, why, and how of each case as well as written releases so that we can contact a psychologist, state board or state association.

Complainee

This is the person, the psychologist (who must be an APA member), being complained about.

Complainant

This is the person who is making the complaint. If the complainant is a non-APA member, there is a five year statute of limitation for making the complaint; if the complainant is an APA member, there is a one year statute of limitation.

Dropped Membership

This is an adjudication which is the most serious one for an infraction of the *Ethical Principles*. When there has been a serious infraction, the Committee will vote Formal Charges (see definition) recommending that a member's membership in the Association be dropped. If that occurs, then that person's name is put on to the annual notification to the membership.

Expulsion

We expel someone when we are taking action contingent upon the action taken by another organization. This can happen when a person is convicted of a felony, is delicensed, or is expelled from a State Association. When we become aware of this action, we will give that person sixty days to show good cause as to why we should not expel him/her. There is confusion between expulsion which is this contingent action as described above and dropped membership which is where we investigate as a possible violation of the ethics code. Both categories are included in the notice to the membership in the Fall.

Formal Charges

When the Committee feels that there has been a serious violation of the ethics code, it moves Formal Charges to the Board of Directors recommending that that person's membership be dropped. The Board of Directors is the only body of the organization which can, in essence, kick someone out. Therefore, the Committee has to go to the Board of Directors recommending that a person's membership be dropped. In dropped membership cases, there is a possibility of a hearing before an independent hearing panel which then will recommend to the Board of Directors. In expulsion cases, the contingency cases, there is no such possibility.

Probation	When the Committee systematically monitors for a named length of time whether a member complies with its requirements (like supervision, treatment, additional training).
Reprimand	A sanction when the code has been broken but there has been no damage to a person. The mildest of the sanctions.
R & P	This is jargon for Rules and Procedures, the due process document which the Committee is bound to follow.
Stipulated Resignation	This is when the Committee, in kind of a plea bargaining manner, negotiates with a complainee (see above) resolution of a complaint wherein the complainee will resign (characteristically in a confidential manner) and agree to certain stipulations, such as not reapplying ever or not reapplying until he/she has engaged in significant rehabilitative efforts.
Sua Sponte	These are cases wherein technically the Committee becomes the complainant because the material which generated the case is in the public domain. This is covered in the R & P's (see above), Section 6.23.
Waiver of the Statute of Limitations	The Rules and Procedures allow the Committee to waive the 5-year time period for a nonmember or the 1-year period for a member to make a complaint. There are three elements involved in the waiver. It has to be a serious allegation which could lead to a dropped membership, there must be good reason for its being made after the time period, and there must be some supporting material for its validity.